Photograhy by Ray Main

rebecca tanqueray

101
IDEAS
kitchens

quadrille

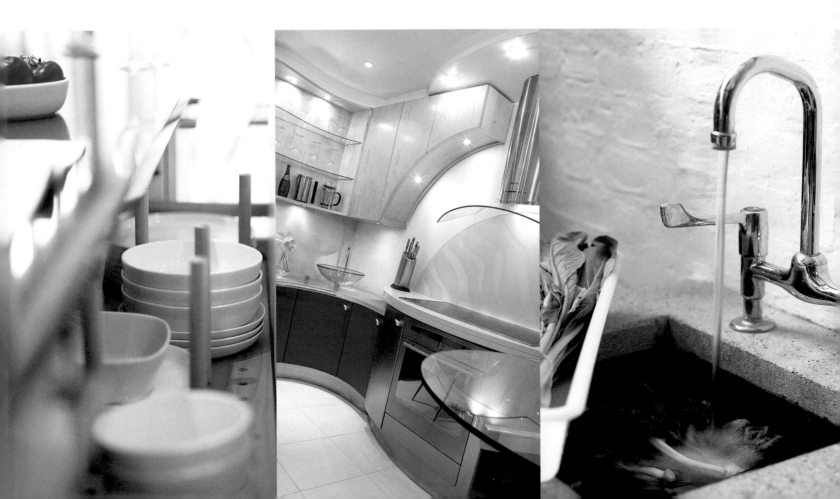

Editorial Director Jane O'Shea
Art Director Helen Lewis
Designer Paul Welti
Project Editor Hilary Mandleberg
Production Jane Rogers

Photography Ray Main

First published in 2004 by
Quadrille Publishing Limited
Alhambra House
27–31 Charing Cross Road
London WC2H 0LS

British Library Cataloguing-in-Publication
Data. A catalogue record for this book is
available from the British Library.

ISBN 1 84400 089 3

Every effort has been made to ensure the
accuracy of the information in this book. In no
circumstances can the publisher or the author
accept any liability for any loss, injury or
damage of any kind resulting from any error in
or omission from the information contained in
this book.

Printed and bound in China.

contents

part one

the big picture

1 where do I start?

Today's kitchen has enormous and divergent demands placed upon it. It needs to be an efficient cooking area with functional appliances and useful surfaces. It needs to be a storage room for crockery, cleaning products, food. Often, it needs to be the laundry-room, accommodating washing facilities and ironing devices. Increasingly, too, the kitchen has become the place where we eat, relax and entertain; somewhere we want to be able to sit down and feel completely at home.

Getting all these things right can seem impossible and when you are revamping or replacing a kitchen, it is tempting to get a kitchen supplier to do it all for you. Buying an off-the-peg fitted kitchen may be the solution, but even if you decide to go down this route, you should always establish exactly what you want first.

five things to do before you begin

1 • Buy specialist magazines and call in brochures to get an idea of the kind of kitchen you want.

2 • Find out from friends or colleagues whose kitchens you like what they did and ask for recommendations of designers, builders and products. Word of mouth is the best endorsement.

3 • Consider your kitchen's shortcomings (too dark, not enough surfaces, etc) and think about how you could improve on it next time around.

4 • Plan what you will do when your kitchen is out of action and establish when the best time would be to start work. Doing without a cooking space is easiest in the summer when you tend to cook less frequently and can eat outside.

5 • Work out how much you can afford to spend and set a budget.

2

ten questions to ask yourself before you begin

mind over matter

is it in the right room?

Relocating a kitchen is a major task, but why make do with a dark and dingy cooking space at the front of the house, when you can create a large open-plan kitchen-cum-dining area at the back? Get professional advice about any structural changes needed and also about moving the utilities. This doesn't cost as much as you might expect (see 9).

can I extend it?

Consider opening up two rooms to make a large kitchen-cum-living area or extending a back kitchen into the garden. You will need professional advice and the work can be expensive but the result will be worth it and should add value to your house.

should I reconfigure the space?

Just by moving the sink or opting for an island unit you might be able to turn an awkward kitchen into a very practical one.

how do I use it?

Is your kitchen just a cooking space or do you like to eat and entertain in it? Analysing the way you use the room can help you to plan everything from the layout to the furniture.

do I need a separate dining area?

If you want to eat in the kitchen, consider how you can divide the cooking and eating areas. It's easy in a large kitchen, but in a small one you will need good planning and careful

design to squeeze it all in (see 13 and 14).

what look do I like?

Farmhouse, Shaker, industrial, – browse through magazines and brochures and pick a look you like. Having a theme in mind will give the project focus and make it far easier to select what you need to buy.

what is my budget?

Knowing how much money you have to spend at the outset is essential and, if you stick to budget, you'll avoid financial disasters.

can I put appliances elsewhere?

Could the washing machine and dryer be stacked on top

of each other in a cupboard? Can the fridge fit in the dining room or under the stairs? Taking a few large appliances out of the kitchen will free up space.

just how much stuff do I need?

If you pare your collection of kitchen possessions down to the bare essentials it will make storage far more straightforward. If you are very short of space, consider storing the things you use rarely (the 'best' china, for example) in another room.

shall I call in the professionals?

It should be obvious if you can tackle your kitchen revamp yourself or if you will need expert help. Remember you can always get help with the planning and design and do the rest yourself (or vice versa).

set a budget

Getting the money sorted out at the start is crucial, so work out exactly how much you have to spend and break it down so you have an individual budget for each aspect of the renovation. Do some research into how much things cost and think about your priorities. You may be prepared to make do with inexpensive units so you can afford a fantastic French range, or you may prefer a good-quality partial refit rather than a sub-standard complete kitchen.

For a big project, factor in the cost of eating out or of creating a temporary kitchen while the original one is out of action. And always allow for delays with builders and supplies. If you have commissioned an architect or building company to do the work for you, make sure you receive a clear breakdown of costs and expect the final figure to be more than the initial quote (a worst-case-scenario rule of thumb is to double a quote to cover the unforeseen).

Also, don't forget to include in your budget the cost of removing your existing kitchen: paying someone to tear out the units, for example, or hiring a skip.

six top budgeting tip

1 • Be realistic: don't set your heart on a high-tech industrial stove if your budget won't stretch to it.
2 • If you are using an architect, don't forget to factor in the fees.
3 • A new kitchen should add to the value of your home, so the cost may be offset by the increase.
4 • If you haven't any spare cash to hand, consider increasing your mortgage to cover the costs. Most mortgage lenders are willing to up loans for home improvements.
5 • Consider how long you will stay in the house. If it's not long, don't spend a lot on things you can't take with you when you go.
6 • To spread the cost, consider splitting the work into two or three phases (although this will prolong the inconvenience, of course).

do I want to use an architect?

If you know just what you want to do to your kitchen and have a recommended builder on hand, there is little point in commissioning an architect. If, on the other hand, that isn't the case, calling in an expert can only make sense. A good architect can advise you about everything from planning permission to the finish of your units and he/she should be able to come up with ingenious and creative solutions to any logistical problems.

Most architects will take on one-room jobs and many also offer a design-only service, which is useful if you already have a recommended builder. But don't automatically expect an architect to project-manage for you; that's something you'll have to pay extra for. To find the ideal architect, ask friends and colleagues for personal recommendations and interview several. An architect will be working very closely with you, so it is important that you are on the same wavelength.

advantages

• An architect will take on all the nitty-gritty, from applying for planning permission, to relocation of utilities, to measuring up the kitchen for units.

• An architectural practice should be able to give you a choice of recommended builders and may also be able to strike a better deal with any of them than you could on your own.

• Architects should be able to offer you a range of creative solutions and ideas for your space, from clever built-in storage to the use of unusual and unconventional materials that you might otherwise not have known about.

disadvantages

• An architect doesn't cost much (their fees are usually around 15% of the total cost of the project) but that bit extra may be more than you can manage.

• Just because you have an architect doesn't mean that the job will go smoothly. Unless you have paid them extra to project-manage the work they often have little more influence with the builders than you do.

• Being caught between an unreliable builder and an over-ambitious architect can be frustrating. Dealing with one party only can be simpler.

5 small budget, big ideas

Having only a little money needn't limit you as much as you might expect. With some lateral thinking and a few good ideas, you can easily turn a grotty kitchen into a chic one without breaking the bank.

five tips to keep costs down

1 • Opt for inexpensive, simple high-street units and splash out on a beautiful worktop instead.

2 • No need to buy new units at all. Simply fit new cupboard doors or just new handles to your existing units.

3 • Source inexpensive but interesting materials for units, worktops and flooring: plywood and even MDF can look sophisticated with a few coats of varnish.

4 • Look in salvage yards: a quirky second-hand sink can make a room.

5 • Use cast-offs ingeniously: wooden pallets stacked up one on top the other, for example, make an impromptu vegetable rack.

6 blow-the-budget kitchens

Having no financial constraints can, perversely, make it harder to know quite where to start with a kitchen refit. Should you splash out on that top-of-the-range cooking system (see 28)? Should you fill the place with bespoke units in solid teak? Should you buy in all the latest appliances and gadgets and turn your kitchen into a temple to high tech? The choice, of course, is a completely personal one but, if you can't decide which route to go down, call in the experts to help. An architect or designer can give you all the options and help to focus your thoughts.

What limitless cash brings you, of course, is the luxury to create a kitchen specially tailored to your needs. Bespoke kitchens can satisfy your every whim from providing you with units custom-made to fit your saucepans to furnishing you with all the extras, such as built-in terracotta bread containers or thermostatically controlled drawers.

If fitted kitchens aren't your thing, spend your money on cutting-edge appliances, specialist wall-finishes or fantastic kitchen furniture: a custom-made refectory table with matching benches, perhaps. Alternatively, reinvent the structure of the room itself. Substitute glass for brick in strategic places to let sunlight flood inside, install a wine cellar beneath the floor or create the ultimate shut-away kitchen by placing everything (including the kitchen sink) behind closed doors. Anything is possible.

five money-no-object tips for your fantasy kitchen

1 • Choose the best materials you can but don't go over the top: subtlety is key.
2 • For ultimate good looks and efficiency, invest in a top-of-the-range fitted kitchen or get units specially made to fit all your possessions.
3 • Change the structure of the room itself. Glass walls and ceilings, for example, will make any kitchen – however small – feel light and spacious.
4 • Treat yourself to fantastic cutting-edge appliances (and make sure you know how to use them).
5 • Get your kitchen (or, indeed your whole house) cabled so that you can invest in the latest integrated lighting, heating and sound system.

7 services

A kitchen would be nothing without water, electricity or gas and it is vital that you sort out their supply before you start on the hard stuff. Unless you are an expert, it is best to call in the professionals both to move services and to fit appliances.

gas

Gas always needs expert installation. Any gas appliance has to be fitted by a registered or licensed dealer/approved contractor to ensure safety.

electricity

Be generous with sockets at worktop level; you are bound to need more than you think and remember, adding extra ones at a later date will be more complicated and more expensive. An electrician will advise you where to place sockets for appliances but, in a fitted kitchen, make sure you will be able to pull the appliance out for maintenance. Don't install sockets near water or sources of heat.

water

Plumbing has become more complicated with the arrival of water softeners (see 56), waste disposal units and steam ovens (some need a direct water supply). Use a plumber who has been recommended and make sure he/she knows exactly what is needed at the outset.

heating

A refit is the perfect opportunity to install extra heating in a kitchen if required. Cutting-edge design vertical radiators work well in a small space but under-floor heating is even better as it gets rid of the need for radiators altogether. It can work with most types of flooring (get professional advice) but you'll need some space under the floor to install it. Under-floor heating can be costly (especially if you have to strip out existing heating first) but gives the luxury of subtle and 'invisible' heat underfoot.

safety 8

Boiling water, sharp knives, gas appliances – the kitchen has lots of potential hazards.

ten ways to make sure your kitchen is safe

1 • Don't place sockets or light switches near the cooker or the sink.

2 • Choose flooring that won't get slippery when wet.

3 • Ensure that no gas appliances leak. Have an old gas cooker checked.

4 • Position a gas hob away from windows and doors: draughts can easily blow out the gas without you realising.

5 • Take sensible fire precautions: fit a smoke alarm, and use non-flammable materials around the cooking area.

6 • Install good lighting: a dimly lit kitchen is a dangerous one.

7 • Make sure there are no jagged corners or sharp edges on worktops or furniture.

8 • Avoid trailing cables: appliance and light flexes must be kept under control.

9 • If you have small children, invest in cupboard locks so that kitchen cleaning products (and food!) are kept out of reach.

10 • Make sure that anything on castors has a locking mechanism so that it can be kept stable.

location, location, location

9

In the past, the kitchen was strictly a utility space and was rarely given the best room in the house. Times have changed, however, and for many of us the kitchen is now the hub of the home. But the kitchens we inherit can be ill-suited to this new multi-purpose role and – if you've the budget – it is worth thinking about relocation.

Consider how you use the room and where it would be best placed – at the front of the house for the morning sun; alongside the garden for easy access for children or pets and to make the home feel more spacious?

If there is no obvious place to put the new kitchen, consider knocking the existing one through to the adjacent room (a rarely used dining room, perhaps) to create a cooking-cum-living space. Or you might link the kitchen to the garden, transforming the connecting wall into a series of

French doors or one giant sliding glass partition. Alternatively, if you spend little time cooking, do without a cooking 'room' altogether and incorporate a new mini-kitchen into an existing living or dining room. Compact one-wall fitted kitchens are becoming increasingly popular (see 19).

Relocating a kitchen is a professional job. The services will probably need to be repositioned (and if you move the drain, you may need planning permission). You may also need to make some changes to the internal layout of the house. Get some quotes; it may not cost as much as you think.

10

five ways to exploit space

big kitchens

1 open planning

Turn the kitchen into the ultimate multi-purpose room with zones for cooking, relaxing, eating and working and fill the space with adaptable furniture (a table you can eat and work at, for example).

2 large furniture

Invest in a huge refectory table to highlight the dimensions of the room without cluttering it. Team it with long, low benches rather than chairs, so the room isn't too busy at eye level.

3 oven envy

Buy a big cooker, or even two for professional looks and stacks of cooking space.

4 create an island

Opt for an island unit (see 21) to make the most of all that central space. It will also allow you to chat with your friends as you cook.

5 relish the space

Paint the room white and put everything behind closed doors for a kitchen that's more installation than utility room. Add a spot of coloured light for instant designer panache.

11

kitchen diners

Making cooking and dining zones work effectively both on their own and together is a hard task. The key is a cohesive decor that doesn't compromise the needs of either area.

kitchen/dining salvation

• If you have knocked a kitchen through into an adjacent dining room, you don't need to make the new space completely open plan. Take down just part of the dividing wall for a connection that doesn't lose the sense of the two individual zones.

• Go for a unified decorative scheme. A squeaky clean white kitchen flowing into a rich red dining room will look disjointed, so try keeping the furniture distinct, but use the same flooring or wall-colouring for both spaces.

• Make the place as practical as you can. Traditional heavy dining room furniture won't work once the room has been incorporated into the kitchen. Simple streamlined pieces throughout are the best bet.

five ways to expand space

12

small kitchens

1 rationalise appliances

Minimise the amount you keep in the kitchen. Appliances can be placed in a cellar or another room; cleaning products can be stored under the stairs; and crockery or glassware may be stacked away in living-room cupboards.

2 avoid eye-level units

Although wall-mounted cupboards will give you extra storage space, they will also make the room seem cramped. Without them, the perimeter of the room will be visible and the kitchen will seem more spacious.

3 wall of glass

Use glass for a kitchen wall or ceiling (check that this is structurally possible first). Having a see-through rather than a solid barrier – even on just one side – will make a small kitchen seem bigger (see 14).

4 clever storage

If you have little room for units, use the walls, the ceiling, even the windows for storage (glass shelves against a window make a brilliant see-through solution). Divide units internally with one or two shelves to give yourself twice the storage space (though make sure your cooking kit still fits). And customise the backs of cupboard doors with narrow shelves (good for spices) and hooks. A long narrow shelf can also be squeezed above the splashback.

5 invisible solutions

Use as many pull-out/fold-away features as you can. Anything that can be 'invisible' when not in use is an asset in a small kitchen.

tiny spaces

Many of us find ourselves cooking in teeny-weeny corridor-like spaces, but there are ways of making even this a pleasure and of creating a mini-kitchen that will function just as well as a maxi one. The key is not to stuff too much into it. Reduce your kitchen kit to the absolute essentials – a cooker, a sink, a fridge – and think of clever ways to incorporate everything else you need.

In a tiny room, fitted kitchens make the best use of the space, so find out what is available. In response to demand, many companies are now offering diminutive kitchens, from designs that incorporate everything along one wall to those that can be shut away inside a cupboard. Clever and compact design doesn't come cheap, of course, but you should get what you pay for.

five ways to make small beautiful

1 • Look around for diminutive appliances. These days it is easy to find smaller-than-standard kitchen kit, from a two-ringed hob to a mini-dishwasher.
2 • Mount as much stuff as you can on the wall (such as the ironing board or microwave) to free up floor space.
3 • Invest in kitchen designs that double up: the sink that can be topped with a chopping board to create an instant worktop, for example. In a small space, everything needs to work twice as hard.
4 • Use any redundant or 'dead' space for storage. Cookery books can be stacked above the fridge; baking kit stored behind the 'kick plates' at the bottom of your units.
5 • Use pull-out rather than swing-door units because they take up less space.

cheat 14
the space

Canny visual tricks can help to make even the smallest kitchen seem bigger than it really is. One of the best is to use glass for one or all of your kitchen walls. A wall-to-wall, floor-to-ceiling window – whether it overlooks a garden or another room – can't help but draw the eye beyond the confines of the kitchen, making it seem more spacious. Creating a glass wall is a major undertaking of course (you will need to call in the professionals) but there are other, less dramatic ways of cheating the space that you can use.

four cheat's specials

1 • Build your units on stilts. Being able to see the floor running underneath will make the room seem less cramped.

2 • Use shiny surfaces. Any reflective material – resin, gloss paint, stainless steel – will give the room depth and increase the sensation of space.

3 • Choose wider-than-average units or cupboards. The result will be to broaden the room visually and also, of course, to give you loads more room for all your oversized pots and pans.

4 • If your kitchen flows into another room, extend the flooring, the wall colouring or even the worktop into the adjacent space. By blurring the boundaries, this will trick the brain into thinking that the kitchen goes further than it really does.

15
make a floor plan

Before you start buying anything for your kitchen, draw a scaled plan of the space on a piece of graph paper. Measure walls and floor; mark any architectural features (windows and doors for example) and also any fixtures and fittings that you wish to keep, making sure that they are all drawn to scale. Be particularly careful to note down the exact position of service points (where the gas comes in, for example), plug sockets and light switches.

Once the plan is complete, you will be able to see at a glance what kind of space you have to work with and what may need to be moved or added to accommodate a new scheme. Now comes the fun part. Using the same scale, make mini-drawings of all the things you wish to put into your new kitchen: appliances, units, furniture (get exact dimensions from suppliers or manufacturers' brochures). Cut these out and then arrange them on the floor-plan both to see if they will fit and also to discover in which permutation they will work best.

It is a good idea, too, to draw a kitchen elevation (i.e. a view from the front) so you can map out the room on the vertical as well as the horizontal.

top tips for the perfect floor plan

• Give yourself alternatives: cut out mini-versions of various different units, for example, to see which works best in the space.
• Remember you are not just trying to make things fit; there must be space for people to use the kitchen and for drawers and doors to open (those that swing take up the most room).
• Once you have decided on a final plan, look at any awkward left-over space and consider what you might do with it: is there room for a cupboard in that corner?; could that gap between the cooker and the units be used for a row of shelves?
• Take several floor-to-ceiling measurements just in case there are discrepancies between one side of the room and the other. Also, when measuring up for a worktop, take the reading at worktop level.

16
ergonomics and work triangles

It is important to ensure that your kitchen is as comfortable as possible to work in, with units and work surfaces at the right height, with sufficient light and with easy access to your equipment.

If you buy a fitted kitchen, a lot of the thinking will have been done for you, but otherwise you need to plan your layout carefully. Think about how you will use the room and arrange appliances and work surfaces accordingly. The ideal, so the experts tell us, is the 'work triangle' – a formula that dictates the optimum distance between cooker, sink and fridge (a total of no more than 6m, apparently). Creating ease of movement between these three prime working spots is obviously the goal, but don't feel constrained by the textbooks: if you want to have your sink at one end of the kitchen and your cooker at the other, go for it (but remember that you will have to carry pots and pans the length of the room).

how to achieve maximum efficiency

• Install the main food preparation area between the sink and the cooker and make sure that there is an unobstructed path between them.

• Don't place the sink or hob in a corner. Not only will this be uncomfortable (you will bang your elbows on the wall), it will also mean you have no useful worktop space at the sides for crockery, cutlery, cooking in progress.

• Position units and gadgets so that you need to do as little bending and stretching as possible: an eye-level grill, for example, is far better than one at worktop height.

• Most worktops come at a standard height, but a kitchen can benefit from the addition of a higher or lower surface, too, especially if you yourself are not a standard height! If you have an island unit, for example, make it lower than the rest to give you a choice of heights to work with.

• In a small kitchen, make sure you leave enough space for the cook! Take the swing- and pull-out factor of doors and drawers into account when you are planning your layout.

17
plan the look

This is the exciting part. Once you've decided on the layout of your kitchen and just what bits and pieces you need, it is time to think about the look of the place. Do you want a rustic country kitchen or a steely modern one? Can you fit an Aga into your scheme for a farmhouse look? Or how about that industrial-style oven? Your budget will obviously come into play here, but think first what style you would like and then – with a little creative thinking – you should be able to come up with ways that you can achieve it. Have a look at what is on offer on the high street and browse through interior magazines for ideas. Remember, you don't have to go for a standard look, you can mix and match shop-bought pieces with your own stuff or customise an off-the-peg kitchen with some brilliant colour or a specially made worktop. Anything goes.

18
make a mood board

If you are not sure quite which look you want, make yourself a mood board. When you see something you like in a magazine or a brochure – whether it's a fantastic appliance or a perfect colour – tear it out and, once you have a collection, pin together on a board or glue onto card. You can include natural things, too: a beautifully coloured leaf, for example, or an attractively textured piece of bark.

Your mood board should make it easy to see what style and colour scheme works best for you (but keep the room's location in mind: dark colours won't do much for a gloomy space). It can also help you eliminate things that don't fit. If your collection of colours and images is mostly traditional it makes rejecting the hyper-modern cooker of your dreams that much easier. If the result is not clear-cut, see what colours and materials dominate and build on them.

five classic layouts 19

The size of the room, the way you use the space and even the dynamics of the family can dictate how you lay out your kitchen. Once you have completed your floor plan (see 15), it may be obvious which arrangement would work best but, if you are not sure, look in kitchen showrooms and interiors magazines to get a feel for what you like.

1 the one-wall kitchen

This is a very neat solution in a small kitchen because everything is contained against one wall. To fit units, appliances and work surface in such a restricted area, however, you will need good planning and tight design. If you have many appliances to accommodate, consider stacking one on top of another in units built

just for the purpose and, if you need a lot of storage space, use eye-level as well as floor units. The sink and the hob can be integrated into the worktop at either end (though not right at the

end) giving you preparation space in between. Even better, create a flap-down worktop that can shut away the sink or the hob (or both) when they are not in use to give you a sweep of uninterrupted surface. For a streamlined look, hide away the entire kitchen 'wall' behind tambour shutters or sliding partitions (useful if the kitchen area forms part of another room).

2 the galley

A favourite with professional chefs, this places rows of units on either side of the room with a corridor in between. It can work well in a small space (as long as you have enough room to move in the middle) and offers an efficient cooking environment with a reasonable amount of worktop and storage space. Make sure that the prime working spots – cooker, sink, preparation area – are far enough apart to allow two people to use the

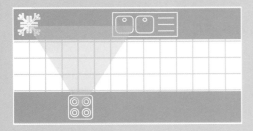

kitchen at once and opt for sliding unit doors to prevent corridor obstruction.

3 L-shapes and peninsulas

Two sides of a triangle already, an L-shape is an ergonomic layout that leaves half of the kitchen free for a dining table. If you have room, create an additional peninsula which extends

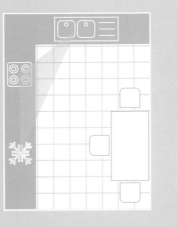

into the central space. This can also function well as an eating space.

4 the U-shape

A popular layout in both small and large kitchens, this will give you lots of storage and work surface but leave little space in the room for anything else. Also, you will need to make sure that the two corners don't become wasted

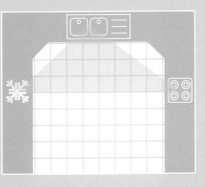

space. Fit them with special extendable corner units (with hinged doors for easy access) and use them for storing things you need irregularly.

5 wraparound units

The ultimate fitted kitchen has units and appliances around all of its walls. In a large space this can leave you room in the middle for a table and make for a sociable, if visually rather functional,

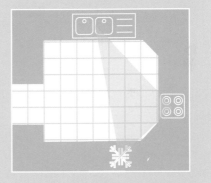

space. In a small space, however, this kind of perimeter kitchen only works if you have enough room in the centre to manoeuvre comfortably. Unless you incorporate a flap-down or pull-out table, it also means you will need to eat elsewhere. Remember, too, that the doors of units and appliances may obstruct each other in a small wraparound kitchen; it is best to place some at eye-level to make access easier.

fitted versus unfitted

20

A fitted kitchen is easy to buy. Any good kitchen company will offer you a range of fixtures and fittings at different prices and in different materials so that you can select a kitchen that fits your budget, circumstances and personal preference. Many will also offer help with planning the layout of the kitchen (whether on computer or in person) and most will fit it for you. With their formula of standard units, off-the-peg fitted kitchens are easy to install and work well in both small and large kitchens. On the downside, however, any fitted kitchen will have that formulaic look about it. It will be structured, functional and utilitarian. Also, once fitted, it is unlikely that you will be able to take any of the elements away with you when you move house.

If you want to create more of a room than a utility space; if your kitchen is a non-standard size or shape; or if you don't want to commit to one particular style, an unfitted kitchen may be a better bet for you. Many good high-street stores now offer quality freestanding pieces, which you can mix and match with your own furniture. Alternatively, if your budget will stretch to it, you could get units specially made for your kitchen in a material of your choice. For an unstructured and very personal look, combine shop-bought units with reclaimed finds – an old butler sink, perhaps, or an old French armoire to use as a larder. Adding unexpected 'non-kitcheny' furniture to the mix will help to make your kitchen feel less utilitarian – an asset if you are planning to use it for dining and entertaining, too.

An unfitted kitchen won't look as streamlined as a fitted one and will probably cost you more (though you can buy bits and pieces gradually rather than all at once), but it can make for a warmer and more interesting space.

advantages of fitted kitchens

- Easy to buy and install
- Makes best use of space in a small kitchen
- Will give a neat and tidy look

advantages of unfitted kitchens

- Will give a more personal, one-off look to your kitchen
- Allows you to mix and match different kinds of furniture
- You can take elements away with you when you move house

21

the benefits of island units no man is an island

If you have the luxury of a large kitchen, consider including an island unit. This will not only make the most of all of the space, it can also take the pressure off the wall-bound units, giving you all the benefits of the perimeter kitchen without the rigid and enclosed wraparound look. An island takes up a fair bit of floor space, so ensure that it is multi-purpose. Use it for appliances, extra work surface, even the kitchen sink; or allow the top of it to overhang at one side to create an informal eating space. For ultimate flexibility (but not if the island contains the cooker or sink), fit it with castors so you can wheel it to one side or, if it is fixed, make it 'float' by placing it on stilts or a pedestal. If you haven't room for an island, buy a large mobile butcher's block, instead.

island advantages

• Can make an effective partition between kitchen and dining area.
• Can accommodate everything from storage cupboards and the kitchen bin

to the cooker or even the sink. Remember, though, that you will need to conceal plumbing and electrics in the legs of the unit and that the service pipes will need to run under the floor.

• With four separate sides, an island can be used by several people at once making it both practical and sociable.
• A floating island – one suspended from the ceiling – can work well in a smaller space, though you need to check with a structural engineer that your ceiling can take the weight.
• Make the top overhang to create an eating area, but ensure there is space for chairs to be slotted underneath.

22 contemporary

It is easy to be contemporary in the kitchen, even if the rest of the house is fairly traditional in style. Being a self-contained and primarily functional space, the kitchen can take on a modern identity without compromising the overall feel of your home and give you the chance to experiment with strong modern lines and up-to-date materials.

fifteen ways to get the look

1 • Opt for clean-lined units and keep them simple. No fussy handles.

2 • Choose sliding unit doors. Swing doors are so 'last century'.

3 • Use glass and stainless steel wherever you can. Frosted glass can also work well as a unit front (see 38).

4 • Choose a chunky worktop – slate, concrete, recycled plastic (see 46–53).

5 • Hide everything behind closed doors. Uncluttered surfaces are key.

6 • A floating island unit in an open-plan kitchen is very contemporary (see 21).

7 • Go for all-white or bold colour.

8 • Keep your walls plain or, if you want pattern, use a textured plaster finish or a retro 1970s wallpaper.

9 • If you opt for wood, make it dark.

10 • Floors should be sleek and unfussy: smooth stone, wide floorboards or a sweep of coloured rubber (see 68–74).

11 • Choose a streamlined sink in steel or stone and dress it up with modern taps (see 55–56).

12 • Buy modern appliances or cover old ones to match your units

13 • Use lighting. Coloured neon tubes will bring your kitchen right up to date.

14 • Remember, less is more. A plain background only needs a splash of the latest colour and a vase of fab flowers.

15 • Fancy a pet? Make it a sleek Weimerana with a chic designer basket!

traditional 23

A warm and cosy traditional kitchen could be just what you need in a cold, urban setting. Look to farmyard and country kitchens for inspiration and even if you can't have the roaring fire or the Aga, you can still get the right feel with a spot of clever decoration.

fifteen ways to get the look

1 • Use natural materials as much as possible. Old wooden boards, worn stone or terracotta tiles on the floor, for example, will give you that comfortable lived-in look.

2 • Opt for an unfitted kitchen if you can: unless you buy at the top of the range, traditional-style fitted kitchens tend to look inauthentic.

3 • Conventional units look inherently modern. Opt for old-fashioned storage instead: a larder, a Welsh dresser or a row of simple wooden shelves.

4 • Uniformity is not what you are after. Idiosyncratic collections of hand-me-down furniture will work brilliantly here.

5 • If you can afford to, invest in an Aga or an old-fashioned range. If you buy new appliances, make them retro-style or conceal modern façades behind tongue-and-groove panelling or a pretty floral curtain.

6 • Avoid steel and glass: hard-edged and modern, they won't work with a traditional look.

7 • Choose old-fashioned furniture: an age-worn kitchen table topped with a gingham or floral tablecloth, for example, or a wooden dresser decked with a collection of mismatched china plates and mugs.

8 • Opt for a butler or Belfast sink and team up with old-fashioned taps.

9 • For the worktop use wood or a slab of time-worn stone. Sleek and uniform granite is not what you want.

10 • A bit of clutter is key in a traditional kitchen, so keep things out on show. Crockery can be arranged on a dresser; baskets of onions, eggs, potatoes, left out on the worktop; jars full of lentils, rice, oats lined up on a shelf.

11 • Hang pots, pans and even garlic and chillies from rails on the ceiling (an old laundry rack would work well).

12 • Dried flowers have become the show-home cliché, but there is always room for fresh flowers. Keep blooms simple and old-fashioned – say a bunch of peonies in a china jug.

13 • Even a traditional-style kitchen needs some modern lighting solutions but keep them subtle and use old-fashioned fittings wherever you can.

14 • An old armchair in a corner (by the fire if you have one or next to the Aga) is the perfect finishing touch.

15 • The pet? A good old black labrador or sheepdog, of course, or a ginger cat.

24 finding people to help

Few but the DIY devotees refit their kitchens single-handedly. However small the room, the jobs involved in creating a new kitchen are effortful and time-consuming: ripping out units; re-laying floors; sorting out the plumbing, electricity, gas. Most of us call in the professionals to help with the nitty-gritty, but finding a good plumber or electrician, can be difficult. Word-of-mouth recommendations are the best, although the Internet is increasingly becoming a useful source with various sites offering contractor referrals and testimonials (though none can be 100% guaranteed, of course). Interview and gets quotes and references from several contractors before you make your choice and make sure they have suitable accreditation.

If you are using an architect or interior designer they should be able to offer you a stable of reliable contractors but first, of course, you have to find them. Again, ask anyone who you know has had a good experience with an architect or designer – or ring up an accrediting body (the Royal Institute of British Architects, for example) who might be able to give you a list of suitable members. Arrange to meet any potential architect in person and ask them to bring samples of their work. This should give you an idea of the area of their expertise and help you to choose which one would be best for the job.

top tips for top people
• Ask around: personal recommendations are best
• Look in the Yellow Pages or on the Internet for suitable companies
• Interview prospective contractors before taking them on
• Always ask for quotes and references

25 order of work

Take a bit of time to establish a clear and accurate schedule before work begins to save complications and time-wasting later.

ten-point checklist
1 • Contact the planning department of your local council if you are planning to extend or change the exterior of your property (if you live in a conservation area there may be tight rules governing what you can and cannot do). If you are altering windows, walls, drains or waste pipes, you will need to get in touch with a building inspector. An architect will sort out any permissions for you.
2 • Decide on the location, layout and look of your new kitchen and remove everything you don't want from the old kitchen (you may need a plumber or electrician to disconnect the sink, hob and oven units).
3 • Set a budget.

4 • Make a plan and order units, appliances, materials (using an architect if you choose to).

5 • Complete any structural work – knocking down walls, damp-proofing, levelling the floor, making holes in the wall for ducting, waste pipes and the like.

6 • Get the services sorted out (plumbing first, usually, and then electricity – but check with the professionals which would be best in your particular situation) and install appliances.

7 • Get any new cabling fitted (though remember to keep telephone cables exposed so that lines can be checked easily in the future).

8 • Paint the ceiling. Doing it at this early stage means it is less likely to get marked when you fit the units.

9• Get the floor laid. If you want the flooring to go underneath the appliances, it can be laid at the start of the project but this will make it prone to damage. Depending on the type of floor you choose, it can also be laid after you fit the units unless you want it to continue underneath them.

10 • Paint the walls; fit the units and worktop;install any plumbed elements sort out the lighting.

the eco kitchen

The kitchen is usually the least eco-friendly room in the house. Appliances eat up energy and water, and we are careless with these resources. On top of that, we use detergents and disinfectants that are full of petrochemicals and phosphates and we fill our bins with non-biodegradable waste.

Whether you are creating a new kitchen from scratch or just going for a revamp, put environmental issues at the top of your shopping list and buy appliances and products that have good eco-friendly credentials.

four essentials for the eco kitchen

1 • Choose eco-friendly materials. Wood is one of the best but ensure it comes from a sustainable source or buy reclaimed boards. Cork and ceramics also have good eco-credentials (as long as they haven't been treated with chemical lacquers and varnishes) and stone and steel rate fairly highly. Avoid plastics unless they are recycled and use plywoods and particleboards sparingly, if at all.

2 • Opt for eco-appliances. These days most come with a rating to show you how efficient and energy-saving they are.

3 • Avoid chemical-based kitchen cleaners. Basic store cupboard items can clean just as effectively and won't pollute.

4 • Minimise packaging. Buy food with as little packaging as possible, avoid plastic packaging and recycle as much as you can.

2

part two

getting down to the detail

appliance science

Today's kitchens need to accommodate more appliances than ever before, so make sure you choose the best available. Browse through design and consumer magazines to find out what is around and remember – looks aren't everything. Any kitchen appliance needs to be efficient, economical, durable, easy-to-clean and as eco-friendly as possible, so do as much research as you can before you buy.

measure up

It is easy to over- or under-estimate the size of your kitchen when you are away from it so before you start looking at the latest lines, measure up the space available for each appliance. Or even better, take a scaled drawing with you when you go shopping so you can see whether a particular product will fit.

built-in or freestanding?

Built-in appliances are generally cheaper than freestanding ones and will give a neat and streamlined look to any kitchen. Remember, however, that a built-in oven will need a separate hob, which will bump the price up, and also that built-in appliances usually need expert fitting (see below). Also, unlike a freestanding range or a separate fridge, it is much harder to take built-in appliances away with you when you move.

can you fit it?

As kitchen appliances become more sophisticated, so fitting them becomes a more complicated process and one best left to the professionals. Today, it is a legal requirement in the UK that any gas appliance be fitted by a registered or licensed contractor and other appliances often need expert handling, especially if they are being built in. Fitted fridges and freezers will need a ventilation gap, for example, and some dishwashers and washing machines will need to be earthed. Get advice from the supplier and call in the experts if you need to.

high tech – low priority

Multi-functional appliances can be impressive but don't be wooed by gadgetry. Extras will always cost you more, so think before you buy whether you really need an oven with eight different cooking settings, for example, or a fridge that gives you crushed ice on tap. High-tech utilities can also over-complicate kitchen life; simple, well-made appliances are usually the best bet.

keep it safe

When it comes to the cooker, safety is a big issue. If you have an old gas cooker, get it checked out by a specialist to make sure it is not leaking and take care when using the hob, particularly if you have young children. Many cookers now come with built-in safety features: heat warning lights for electric plates and automatic re-ignition and shut-off devices for gas rings, for example.

big may not always be best

Increasingly popular, giant industrial cookers and catering fridges can look great in a large kitchen and buying from shops which supply the trade can save you money. Before you commit yourself, though, check that any catering appliance will function as effectively on a domestic scale as it does on a commercial one. A vast industrial cooker may need a larger-than-standard gas pipe, for example; a fridge meant for a restaurant kitchen may make far too much noise in a domestic one. Check out all the nitty-gritty with the manufacturer or supplier or opt for the safer bet and buy a 'catering-style' appliance on the high street.

instant camouflage

If you can't afford the latest, cutting-edge appliances, opt for the standard models and customise them. Hide boring white façades behind closed doors or cover them up with a sleek panel of stainless steel or wood veneer (you may need to get this custom-made although some manufacturers offer a variety of different frontages for their products). A less costly option is to use sticky-backed plastic as a cover up (choose one that can withstand high temperatures if it is being used for a dishwasher or oven).

slimline for small spaces

If you have a tiny kitchen, you don't need to go without the latest appliances. Most products today come in slimline versions that can squeeze into even the smallest spaces. There are also a host of space-saving and convertible appliances on the market: the sink that turns into a dishwasher, for example, or the flip-up hob that can be folded against the wall when not in use. Send off for manufacturers' brochures and ask in stores about forthcoming ranges. There are more options than you might imagine.

think eco

All kitchen appliances eat up energy and waste water but some are less wasteful than others. Most products on the market are now marked with an environmental rating so that it is easy to distinguish which are the most eco-friendly. Look for the EU Eco label in Europe or the Green Seal or Energy Star label in the USA.

intelligent appliances

Coffee makers that can be switched on by the alarm clock; mixers that can weigh ingredients as they are put in the bowl; ovens that will turn on automatically – intelligent appliances are no longer a pipe dream. And you don't even need to have your whole house cabled to enjoy all this. Most new technologies enable appliances to 'talk to each other' using existing electrical wiring. Ask your local supplier for details or take a look on the internet. The cooker that can whizz up a meal for you in your absence may not be as far away as you might think.

28

which cooker?

Where would a kitchen be without a cooker? It's the key appliance and one we need to get right above all the others. Think carefully about the kind of cooker that will suit you: gas or electric; a big old-fashioned range or a built-in cooker with a separate hob? Your choice will largely depend on budget, space and personal preference, of course, but it is also a good idea to look in consumer magazines for performance ratings and details of the latest technological advancements.

standard freestanding

The cheapest option of all is to buy a simple one-oven cooker with an integral hob. These used to come in a standard 60cm width but wider versions are now available. Before you buy make sure that the oven is big enough for your needs (the internal capacity should be shown alongside the external dimensions) and note that self-cleaning ovens usually have less cooking space inside. Buy an oven with glass doors if possible. They are easy to clean and allow you to monitor your cooking inside.

agas and rayburns

Classics of the country kitchen, these enamel-finished cookers are extremely heavy and need a solid supporting floor. They can run on gas, oil, electricity or solid fuel and their hot plates and ovens are heated constantly. Devotees swear that they perform better than any modern stove. They are not cheap but should last a lifetime and may heat your home and/or water to boot.

catering-style cookers and french ranges

These top-of-the-range appliances offer fantastic cooking capacity: two or more multi-function ovens, five or six gas rings, integral grills and griddles, for example. You might even get warming drawers, wok stands and rotisserie facilities. Freestanding, they

are reasonably heavy and need a strong floor. A favourite with professional cooks, they cost big money, though less-expensive scaled-down versions are on the increase. Useful extras include hanging rods for utensils and integral lights.

built-in oven and separate hob

The most popular option today, a built-in oven with separate hob allows you to create two different cooking areas and also to position your oven wherever you like (at waist or eye-level, for instance). These types of oven are more costly than a standard freestanding one but also more convenient and flexible.

29 extraction

These days, most of us tend to cook more on top of the stove than inside it. With little time to bake, we opt for stir-fried suppers whizzed up in a wok or simple meat, fish or vegetables char-grilled on a griddle. Our kitchens, therefore, are often steamier, smokier and smellier than ever before and adequate and effective ventilation is vital. Lingering cooking fumes and moisture are not just unpleasant to live with, they can also damage the fabric of the kitchen – vinyl tiles or wood veneers, for example, will start to lift in a humid environment.

Top-of-the-range cookers come with their own matching hoods and extractor fans, but standard cookers may not, in which case it is worth buying your own. An open door or window just won't give you the ventilation you need. Various models of fan are available, so get advice from the supplier as to which will suit your kitchen best (note that he or she will need to know the volume of the room in cubic metres to establish just what level of extraction you will need). And also rate the unit for noise. Some

extractor fans (particularly worktop-mounted designs that pull air down rather than up) can be very noisy, which may cause annoyance.

The most efficient extractor fans are those fitted directly to an outside wall but this is not always a possibility. If you need a ducting channel, try to make it as short and straight as possible for maximum efficiency. Standard white ducting is ugly, so it might be worth creating a false ceiling to hide it (if you have no space above the existing ceiling, that is). For a more industrial look, leave your ducting on show, but cover it with something more aesthetic: stainless steel, perhaps, or a piece of anodised aluminium tubing.

If you have no access to an outside wall, opt for a re-circulation unit instead, which filters and refreshes the air before pumping it out again into the room. Though not as efficient as a ducted extractor fan, this can be adequate for a small, infrequently used kitchen.

which hob?

30

Gone are the days when a hob meant four electric hot plates; today there are all kinds of cooking facilities on the top of the cooker – griddles and wok stands, mini two-burners or vast six-ringed ranges, hobs with integral deep fat fryers and pan rests.

If you are buying a separate hob, choose one that will suit your cooking style and kitchen (materials are various: glass, stainless steel, enamel) and think which will work best for you practically. If you have a narrow worktop, for example, opt for a new-style hob with four cooking zones in a row; if you are left-handed, pick a hob with controls at the front rather than at the standard right-hand side so that you won't need to reach across the heat to control the burners. Make sure, too, that you have a range of ring sizes to accommodate different saucepans.

When it comes to the choice between gas and electric, the differentials are narrowing. While gas used to be easier to control, new halogen or induction heating comes close to providing the same kind of service as gas, giving fast heat and quick switch off.

Whichever fuel you choose, much of the hob-top cooking we do today – stir-fries and griddle cooking – will cause smells, steam and smoke, so good ventilation in the form of an extractor fan or cooker hood is essential (see 29).

more cooking choices

the microwave

The microwave has revolutionised home cooking. Great for speed cooking and relatively easy to use and clean, it is a useful companion to the conventional cooker and sometimes completely takes its place. Shop around to see which power level and capacity suits you best. A compact microwave is fine for defrosting or warming small amounts of food but would be insufficient for a family meal.

They take up a lot of worktop space, so consider getting one built in, otherwise make sure that any unit looks good in your kitchen. Recent developments have seen microwaves fitted with browning units or combined with conventional ovens for that 'total cooking experience'. In both cases, the units will be more costly and take up more space.

top tips for choosing a microwave

• A turntable will help to ensure an even distribution of heat but will eat up internal space: removable turntables are the best bet.
• Electronic touch controls are more user-friendly than manual ones (though the latter will cost less) and also offer a range of automatic cooking programmes.

the steam oven

The latest innovation to hit the high street, the steam oven offers a new, quick and healthy way of cooking. Manufacturers claim that no fats or oils are required and that flavours are quickly sealed in and don't mix. Smaller than a conventional cooker, a steam oven can be built in to your kitchen units or placed on a worktop. The newest work with an internal water reservoir and don't need to be plumbed in. This type of oven is expensive and not suitable for baking.

refrigeration

One of the key components of the kitchen, the fridge comes in all shapes and sizes. To help you choose, consider how much you need to store in it. If you buy a lot of fresh food, you'll need a fridge with a large capacity. If, on the other hand, you use dried and tinned food more frequently than fresh, a small under-the-counter fridge will be adequate.

five tips to help you choose

1 • Decide whether you want a fridge on its own or a fridge-freezer. If you opt for a combined fridge-freezer, make sure that the fridge is at eye-level and the freezer is beneath as you will need to access the fridge far more often.

2 • Non-standard catering-style fridges are becoming fashionable. If you do go down this route, however, make sure you check out the noise factor before you buy. In a domestic setting a commercial fridge can be deafening.

3 • If you are thinking of moving house in the not-too-distant future, buying a freestanding fridge that you can take with you when you go is the best choice.

4 • Think eco: buy a model that is low-energy and noise rated (A is best, G is worst) and free of harmful CFCs. Also, keep your fridge well stocked and don't leave the door open.

5 • It is easy to be wooed by the extras, such as iced water and crushed ice dispensers, but consider just how much you will use them before you commit yourself.

dishwashers and laundry

dishwashers

A modern luxury, dishwashers are now commonplace. They come in standard sizes and are generally fitted into the run of wall units to give a streamlined result. Some are available in a choice of finishes, but if you can't find one you like, conceal it behind a panel that matches the rest of your units – though make sure it is still easy to load and unload. Most dishwashers will hold enough for five full place settings, so if you live alone it might be best (and more eco-friendly) to invest in a slimline version or smaller. Two-drawer dishwashers are now available as well as 'in-sink' designs, which fit ingeniously inside the bowl of the sink when needed. These designs also work well in a tiny kitchen where space is limited.

To choose the right brand, browse through consumer magazines (most do frequent product surveys) and ask around, but note that with most modern machines any differences of noise, speed and efficiency are fairly negligible.

washing machines and dryers

Ideally, these will not be in the kitchen itself: even supposedly quiet machines can be disruptively noisy. But if there is nowhere else, conceal them in a kitchen cupboard and place as far away as possible from the main centre of activity. A layer of foam or rubber underneath can help reduce noise and vibration levels. If you don't have space for two machines, consider a combined washer-dryer but bear in mind that the washing capacity of these is usually far less than that of a standard machine.

four tips to help you choose

1 • Go for the most eco-friendly versions available. They should all be labelled with an energy rating but ask the supplier or retailer for information if this is not explicit. Also, avoid running any of them half-empty.

2 • Check out the noise factor before you buy – particularly if your kitchen is small.

3 • Look in consumer magazines to discover the current best performers and ask friends for recommendations.

4 • Don't be wooed by gadgetry. Often the simplest machines are the best.

storage special

34

Storage is a particular challenge in the kitchen as we need to accommodate a huge array of diverse equipment: crockery, cleaning kit, glassware, table linen, food. Assess just what you need to store and then think how you would like to do it. Do you want built-in units or freestanding furniture? Do you want to hide everything behind closed doors or keep things out on show on open shelving? Do you need lots of space for store-cupboard food or can you keep most of your weekly shop in the fridge? The storage options available are many and varied, so look around to see what will suit you and your budget best.

fitted or unfitted?

Fitted kitchens use a formula of storage units with a few optional extras, such as pull-out units for bins and extendable corner units. Though you will be able to choose from a range of finishes, fitted kitchen units come in standard sizes so may not be the best option for an awkwardly shaped kitchen. Freestanding pieces will not give you the streamlined finish of a fitted kitchen, but can look more individual. Many high-street shops are now selling good freestanding ranges.

unexpected storage

In a small kitchen, especially, exploit every bit of space. Turn an unused alcove or an old chimneybreast into a cupboard and use the 'dead' space above the fridge or between appliances for cookery books or trays. Even the

space between the bottom of your units and the floor can be used for baking kit or tea towels. Fit drawers with a push mechanism here, so that you can open them with your feet.

which units?

Even fitted kitchens now offer a range of styles. Units on legs, for example, are fashionable and functional and also increase the sense of space. They work well on uneven floors and make cleaning easier. Units with pull-down tambour shutters will give your kitchen cutting-edge kudos, while extendable corner units will give you access to awkward storage spaces.

paring down

If you are serious about getting some order into the kitchen, pare your equipment down to the essentials. Don't

hang onto that fondue set you never use (and never will) and store that wedding cruet set somewhere else if you must keep it. A core collection of crockery and kitchen kit is easier both to store and to maintain.

storage wall

If you have a sizeable kitchen, why not convert one entire wall into a floor-to-ceiling storage area? Look around for a system that will suit or get one made to your own specification. A chequerboard of open storage boxes works well if you like your tableware and foodstuffs on show, while a series of floor-to-ceiling cupboards is neat and streamlined. If you can't decide which to go for, do both, mixing closed units at the bottom with open shelves on top. A storage wall will provide you with lots of space and, paradoxically, will seem far less obtrusive than an array of separate cupboards and shelves.

decorative doors

Even in a contemporary kitchen you don't need to opt for plain unit fronts. Bespoke doors can be produced in any size and with interesting creative effects. Try mixing and matching different woods for the frame and the central panel, for example; use gloss and matt paint in the same tone in sequence around the kitchen or clad the doors with steel, zinc or even copper.

practically perfect

Units are there to provide a service, so make them as practical as possible. To make access easier opt for pull-out units or lift-out baskets if you haven't much space; line shelves with rubber or waxed paper matting to stop crockery sliding around; choose deep or extra-wide drawers to accommodate large pots and pans. Think, too, about the location of your storage. After all, you don't want food cupboards right next to the oven.

can you handle it?

For a clean-lined modern look, you want sleek and simple door handles or, even better, no handles at all. Instead, pierce a finger hole in the unit front; use push-open latches or leave a lip at the bottom of high-level unit fronts for easy opening. Alternatively, go for the modern option of sliding unit doors. Doing away with the swing-factor will save you space but, remember, you won't have access to all your cupboards at once.

ceiling storage

If you have a high ceiling, make the most of it. Erect a hanging rack for pots, pans, sieves and colanders (see 40). Stick to the ironmongery, though; colourful plastics will look out of place. Also, make sure your equipment does not end up out of reach. A pulley system will allow you to vary the height of the hanging rack when necessary.

make it individual

Don't feel you have to buy strictly functional furniture for the kitchen; the addition of a more decorative or quirky piece can make all the difference: instead of a built-in larder, for example, use an old French armoire for storing food or buy an old hotel trolley to make a quirky shelving system. Individual details like this will give your kitchen far more character than a run of identikit units.

35

wood/veneer unit fronts

Wood is a popular choice for kitchen units. Natural, warm and available in many different varieties, it is also a perfect material for construction. Top-of-the-range kitchens have made-to-measure units in solid wood that will have been acclimatised to the indoor environment to prevent warping; mid-range kitchens offer timber doors fitted to hardboard or MDF carcasses; inexpensive chain-store kitchens substitute veneered doors for solid wood.

Design is largely a matter of personal taste and budget. Tongue-and-groove will give you a classic, country look; beaded and framed doors, a hint of Shaker style; smooth panels, a sleek contemporary feel. Browse through magazines and brochures to get an idea of what you like and get quotes from high-street dealers or from independent kitchen companies. You will almost certainly be spoilt for choice.

advantages

• Looks good with stainless steel, glass or stone worktops
• Can soften the hard-edged look of a contemporary kitchen
• Easy to clean: wipe down with a just-damp cloth or use mild detergent for more stubborn stains
• Can be stained or repainted to give the room a revamp
• Grainy woods bring instant pattern to a bland utility space
• Comes in many varieties of colour and texture
• Flexible veneers can be used for curvy cupboard fronts

disadvantages

• An all-timber look can be overpowering so avoid wooden floors and worktops if units are timber, too
• All solid wood will warp in a centrally heated home so cupboards must be properly constructed to counteract this
• Custom-made wooden carcasses may last but will be expensive
• Cheap wooden veneers are not particularly durable and may need to be replaced after a couple of years

laminate and painted unit fronts

Cheap and practical, laminate is ideal for kitchen cupboards. It comes in virtually any colour or pattern (including wood or stone effect) and is very easy to keep clean. You can even get mirrored Formica, which does wonders for the light. Though not as durable as solid wood, good-quality laminate should last well. The favoured choice of many a high-street kitchen shop, laminate units are easy to come by, but you can have non-standard sizes or shapes made to order.

Paint is the most flexible of all finishes and can do much to brighten up a dull kitchen. Wooden or hardboard units can be transformed with a new colour and these days, it is easy to find specialist paints for covering up everything from metal to laminate and tiles. A spray-painted or lacquered finish will be more uniform than a brushed one. Paint comes in countless colours and several finishes. High gloss is a current favourite. It is very easy to clean and maximises natural light.

advantages

• Laminate comes in hundreds of colours and patterns, from stripes to wood grain
• Laminate is inexpensive and easy to clean
• Paint is inexpensive and easy to use and works on most existing surfaces
• Most paints, particularly gloss or enamel finishes, are easy to wash down
• Paint is available in countless colours and finishes, from high gloss to metallic

disadvantages

• Standard laminated units can look formulaic: it's worth paying more for a great colour or a made-to-order design
• Laminate probably won't last a lifetime
• If scratched or knocked, paintwork will chip: units may need a fresh coat of paint every year or so

metal unit fronts

37

Perfect for the industrial kitchen look, metal is a firm favourite in the domestic kitchen and stainless-steel units are now available across the board from top-quality designer kitchens to more affordable high-street versions. They can be expensive but are also durable, hygienic and fairly easy to keep clean. Metal is also useful for creating units in non-standard shapes. Because it is pliable, it is perfect for cladding the curved contours of an island unit, for example.

advantages

- Will give a sleek, industrial look to any kitchen
- Pliable and useful for cladding curved surfaces
- Shiny stainless steel is very reflective and will help maximise natural light
- Works particularly well with glass or wooden worktops
- Comes in many varieties and textures: matt for a cool contemporary feel; punched or embossed for a Shaker look
- Steel carcasses are solid and strong: perfect for supporting that heavy concrete worktop

disadvantages

- Usually more expensive than wood
- Shows marks easily (clean with a lightly oiled cloth to bring up the shine)
- Can look hard and utilitarian if not tempered with colour or a softer material such as wood

38

glass unit fronts

Glass makes great see-through storage wherever it is used in the kitchen. Glass shelves set against a wall look less obtrusive than wooden ones and, in a small room, a series of these set against a window will create good display space without cutting out the light (you'll probably need to get them custom made, though).

Using glass in the fronts of units is a popular contemporary choice (you will need to make sure it's toughened) and will give a lighter feel to a room than solid wood. Choose a finish you like (frosted, ribbed, wired) or leave clear to create a window onto your tableware, glasses or even food. Such units work particularly well at eye-level and become more of a feature if they are lit from the inside.

advantages
• Being transparent, glass is less obtrusive than more solid materials – a bonus in a small room
• The stuff of the modernist movement, it gives any kitchen contemporary kudos
• Easy to clean
• Comes in many finishes and textures, from frosted to ribbed to tough wired glass

disadvantages
• The sharp corners of glass shelves and units can be hazardous: edges should always be ground smooth and corners rounded
• Custom-made glass pieces will be expensive

39

curtaining

Inexpensive and quick to make, curtains are a good ad-hoc concealing solution and can give your kitchen an appealingly retro look. Use them to hide cluttered shelves or open storage or even to cover up an ugly appliance. Create panels in whatever fabric you like (a pattern with a 'kitchen' theme such as crockery or cooking can work particularly well); hook or thread onto curtain wire and attach under the lip of your worktop or onto the sides of the storage unit. Choose washable fabric or opt for something more original: plastic sheeting, for example, or waxed cloth.

advantages
• Easy to swap when you feel like a change
• Inexpensive
• Can add a decorative flourish to a bland utility space

disadvantages
• Won't give a sleek and streamlined look to the kitchen
• Fabric will get dirty quickly

storing cooking equipment

Saucepans, frying pans, woks, juicers, blenders, rice cookers . . . all of us these days have stacks of kitchen equipment and, unless we store it effectively, it can overtake the room. While it makes sense for some gadgets to be left out on the worktop (the toaster, for example), why allow something you use rarely to eat up valuable preparation space? Having a medley of differently designed bits and pieces on show will also make the kitchen look cluttered and untidy. Once you have pared down your collection of kitchen kit (see 34), assess how much and what kind of storage you need. The options are endless but here are some ideas.

pots and pans

These are notoriously difficult to store. Consider using wider-than-average cupboards (or a two-cupboard unit) placed near the cooker. Both are a good solution, but be sure that you don't overfill them. You need to be able to see and access what you want easily. And remember, a medial shelf will double the storage space and make for a more organised cupboard. If your kitchen has a high ceiling, consider erecting a rack or series of rails and hang saucepans, frying pans, colanders and sieves from them (see 34).

baking kit

If you are a keen cook, store basins, measuring jugs and cake tins somewhere close to hand; if not, keep them on a high shelf or at the back of a corner cupboard so they won't get in the way. Use a separate container for smaller items (for example, biscuit cutters, piping bags) so that they don't clutter up your drawers. Store baking trays and wire racks at the base of the cooker or find a space to stash them vertically so that you haven't got to rifle through all of them to get to the one you need.

big stuff (blenders, juicers)

Streamlined blenders look good left out on the worktop (if you have space); cumbersome, unattractive gadgets are best kept hidden. Store on a high shelf if you use them infrequently and keep the extras (cutters, beaters, blades or whatever) in an old plastic storage container alongside. Fit pull-out drawers or baskets inside your units to make order and access easier.

toasters and kettles

Well-designed appliances can be left out on show if you have the space. If not, store in a unit at the same level as the worktop to avoid constant bending or stretching.

small stuff (spoons, ladles, knives)

A rail attached to the cooker or splashback can be useful for slotted spoons, ladles, garlic crushers, tea strainers, and so on. Keep like with like. Store wooden spoons, spatulas and pastry brushes together, perhaps in an open jar and attach cooking knives to an easy-to-reach magnetic strip fitted above the work surface.

chopping boards

Slot neatly between or behind other gadgets or fit an integral board into your worktop or over the sink – a great way of hiding those dirty dishes.

storing food

41

However little we cook, our kitchens are always full of food. There are store cupboard items (coffee, tea, flour for instance); vegetables and fruit; fresh meat and ready-meals; herbs and spices. Each category needs its own storage spot and it can be a challenge to know quite where to put it. The key is to make maximum use of the space you've got and to make your food storage work for you. Store similar things together; label jars and boxes clearly; and keep things you use frequently to hand. Most importantly, have regular clear-outs and discard anything that is out of date or past its best.

the larder

A traditional walk-in larder is ideal. Cold and capacious, it can house everything from baked beans to yesterday's roast chicken. If you haven't the luxury of one, use a floor-to-ceiling unit that backs onto an outside wall and fill it with shelves. If you are restricted to ordinary units, use them logically: keep one for baking ingredients, another for pasta and rice, and so on.

the fridge

The big American-style fridge has in some ways taken over the role of the old-fashioned larder. Though it's not the place for dry goods, it can accommodate a wealth of fresh produce and also some store-cupboard essentials (pesto or tomato puree for example) to take the pressure off the kitchen units. Even a small fridge, kept well organised, should have room for jams and preserves.

shelves

Though most of us hide our food behind closed doors, open storage can work well and help to give a visual break from all the hard, shiny surfaces of a streamlined modern kitchen. Make any food display graphic and eye-catching: line up cans of soup in a row, for example, or group together a collection of interesting olive-oil bottles. Baskets of hardy vegetables (onions or red peppers, say) or glass jars full of pasta or cereal also look good kept on show and free up unit and fridge space. If you have little room, consider fixing narrow shelves to the back of unit doors. Using what would otherwise be wasted space, these are perfect for herbs and spices.

wine racks

If you don't have a cellar, where do you put the wine? Most kitchen manufacturers supply purpose-built wine-storage units, which can be incorporated into the structure of a kitchen. If you are not buying off-the-peg, place racks in the 'dead' space at the top of your wall-mounted units, perhaps, or even behind the kick plates at the bottom.

42
storing crockery, glassware and cutlery

How you choose to store your crockery, glass and cutlery depends on how you like your kitchen. If you favour minimalism then everything will need to be stowed behind closed doors, but if you prefer a more lived-in look and enjoy having your possessions on show there is great decorative potential in open storage. Whatever you choose, keep your tableware well ordered so that it is easy to find what you need and don't hold onto things that are damaged or that you no longer use.

crockery

Store plates, bowls and cups separately if you can and don't stack them too high if you wish to avoid breakages. Open storage can work well: a uniform collection of white china lined up on a shelf will look smart and graphic (though it will get dusty if not used frequently). If you have a Welsh dresser or long shelf, consider displaying an assortment of different plates and fix hooks to the shelf-edge to accommodate cups and mugs. Alternatively, allot one unit (or two if necessary) for all your crockery (close to the dishwasher for easy unloading) and keep the things you use most frequently at the front. Occasionally used 'best' china should be kept apart on a high shelf or in another room.

cutlery

An assortment of different cutlery can make a mess of any kitchen drawer. Sort it by type and invest in drawer dividers to establish order. Top-of-the-range fitted kitchens offer special drawers for cooking knives but a wall-mounted magnetic strip or a wooden block on the worktop works just as well (see 40). Remember, whatever you choose needs to be safe and easily accessible. For other cooking cutlery (ladles, serving spoons, garlic crushers), a rail attached to the splashback or the cooker hood can be useful (but fix it to one side of the hob to avoid a build-up of grease and to prevent burns).

glassware

The most breakable tableware of all, glass should be stored especially carefully. Keep it at eye-level if possible so that you can access it easily and – if you choose open storage – be prepared to wash the dust off before use. Glass on glass can make a brilliant see-through display, so consider erecting glass shelves for your tumblers, flutes and glass bowls. Everyday glass should be kept close at hand; party glasses can be stored separately at the back of a cupboard or on a high shelf.

43
storing tall, thin and challengingly shaped stuff

If you don't have the luxury of a cellar or an 'under-the-stairs' cupboard, all the cleaning and laundry paraphernalia ends up in the kitchen. Make sure you incorporate a tall unit into the room scheme right at the start to accommodate mops, brooms and the ironing board and set it as far away from the main cooking space as you can. If yours is an unfitted kitchen, make use of awkward corners or shallow spaces for this kind of storage. Another neat space-saving solution is to hang long-handled items (and even the ironing board) from hooks attached to the back of a cupboard door.

If you have no spare vertical space, consider horizontal storage. A mop and a broom don't take up much lateral space after all. They could even be stashed behind the kick plates of your units, although you may need an extra cupboard for bulkier items, such as buckets and vacuum cleaners.

44
eight space-saving storage solutions

The kitchen has to accommodate a wealth of equipment and keeping it clutter-free can seem an unattainable goal. With careful planning, good organisation and a spot of ingenuity, however, you can find a home for everything.

1 • Use every bit of available space for storage: above the units; on top of the fridge; at the base of the cooker; behind the kick-plates; even in front of a window. Dead space is wasted space, so turn it into storage.

2 • Mount as much as you can on the wall to free up floor space

3 • Use the backs of unit doors for storage

4 • Choose pull-out rather than swing-door units to save space

5 • Invest in expandable racks to extend the capacity of your units

6 • Rather than having a drawer above each of your units, stack them on top of each other in just one carcass. This will give you more space and flexibility in the other units.

7 • Buy a diverse collection of units to suit your needs: doubles for pots and pans, singles for crockery.

8 • Remember that cupboards that 'float' off the floor don't seem so obtrusive.

top tips for difficult storage

• Wall-mount your ironing board behind the main door or hang from hooks on the back of the larder to free up floor and cupboard space.

• Use awkward corner spaces for vacuum cleaners and cleaning equipment.

worktops that work

The worktop is one of the hardest working surfaces in the kitchen. Constant preparation area and sometimes chopping board, it is subjected to knocks, scratches, water and food spills. In an ideal world it should be stain- and scratch-proof and very easy to clean. The worktop is also, however, the most visible part of our units so we also want it to look good. Choose a material you like (and can afford) and weigh up its pros and cons. If you are desperate to have a sleek sweep of glossy glass, you must be prepared to protect its surface with pot stands and separate chopping boards, or you may prefer a laminated worktop you can simply wipe clean to a solid wood worktop, which will need a fair bit of after-care. Before you make your final choice, make sure you have got all the necessary information about fitting and upkeep from the supplier.

sealing the surface

Whatever material you choose, it is likely that it will need to be sealed before use. Before you buy, check with the supplier what treatment your worktop needs and whether a sealant will last a lifetime or need to be reapplied regularly. Timber needs to be lacquered or oiled fairly frequently (see 46). Most pre-cut stone comes ready-sealed, but if you buy reclaimed slabs, you may need to seal them yourself.

top heavy?

Granite, concrete and glass are weighty materials and need strong support underneath. Get advice from the supplier or a structural engineer and, if in doubt, choose a lighter material, such as slate or stainless steel.

cutting out

Remember that a worktop is usually interrupted by sinks, taps and pipes. While Corian (see 53), wood and laminate can accommodate cut-out sections fairly easily, fitting is more difficult, and often more expensive, with brittle and inflexible materials such as stone or glass. Make sure that a template for the worktop is mapped out very precisely, particularly if it is being made off-site. If the hole for the sink is out by just a few centimetres, the entire length will have to be replaced.

where to put the sink?

Before choosing your worktop material, think what kind of sink you want: integrated, undermount or drop-in (see 55). An integrated sink will only work with waterproof materials, such as Corian or stainless steel. An undermount or drop-in sink will work with any worktop material.

eating on the worktop

If your kitchen flows through into another room, why not carry the worktop on beyond the base units, to form a peninsula eating area? This is a neat solution to the

problem of accommodating a dining table. Remember, though, that a worktop isn't always the same height as a conventional table; you may need taller-than-standard chairs or stools with it.

how low can you go?

Most fitted floor units come in a standard size, so the worktop, too, will usually be at a fixed height. If you have space for more than one work surface, vary the heights for greater flexibility. A lower counter-top can be very useful for smaller adults and for children; it can also make certain kitchen tasks – kneading or rolling out pastry – far easier. And by introducing different levels you will make the kitchen look less formulaic.

formica

Formica, invented in 1913, is probably the best-known laminate around and has been adopted for cafés and domestic spaces worldwide. Superseded today by various high-tech equivalents, Formica has a certain vintage cachet, but still functions effectively as a wipe-clean, low-maintenance surface.

two in one

Think what materials will work best for the tasks you want to perform on your worktop. Cool marble, stone or glass are perfect for pastry- and sweet-making; wood is good for slicing and chopping; stainless steel is heat-proof and easy to clean. Consider a combination worktop to give yourself the best of both worlds. A worktop comprising a long sweep of stainless steel around the hob and an area of wood block at one end is practical and good-looking.

be creative

Just because you want a practical worktop doesn't mean it has to be dull. Have it overhang your units and give it a curvy edge, for example (though with some materials there will be more wastage, see 57) or make it out of an unexpected material. One colourful, eco-friendly option uses recycled plastic. Made of old shampoo and detergent bottles, it looks like synthetic marble and comes in various different colourways, depending on its content.

don't forget the edges

It is easy to think about the top of your work-surface and to forget that the profile will be on show, too. And the chunkier your worktop is, of course, the bigger the profile will be. For a worktop in a solid material, such as wood or stone, various edge designs are available. Choose one that gives you a smooth finish for safety's sake: sharp corners can be a hazard, especially if there are children in the house. Laminated or tiled worktops will need a separate edging. Consider using a contrasting material, or setting the entire worktop inside a wooden frame.

wooden worktops 46

Wooden work surfaces have shaken off their scrubbed kitchen table image and now that timber is being sourced from all over the world, some very durable woods are available (though avoid buying endangered tropical hardwoods if you can: a Forest Stewardship Council (FSC) label marks out wood from a sustainable source). Wooden worktops need to be sealed to protect them from humidity (particularly in centrally heated homes) and can be either finished with a lacquer, which should be reapplied each year, or oiled every two to three months. Oiled wood is tougher and more resistant to heat marks than lacquered wood and it also improves with age. Another option is to use end-grain wood (i.e. wood that has been turned on end and glued together in blocks). This has the look of a chopping board, is less liable to warp and makes a good cutting surface. Varnished plywood (glued together in layers to give a stripy profile) can also make a good and very reasonably priced worktop. The cost varies according to the type of wood and application: generally speaking, the more hardwearing the wood, the higher the cost.

advantages
• The huge variety of woods means great potential for creativity: a wooden worktop can look dark and luxurious (stained oak works well or wenge – if you can find it from a sustainable source); warm and honey-coloured (reclaimed teak, maple) or pale and interesting (beech, elm, spruce).
• It is warm, mellow, natural and improves with age
• It can be used to soften the hard edges and shiny finishes of stainless steel and glass and will also add warmth to a cool white kitchen.

• Can be installed by a proficient amateur
• Reasonably good at absorbing kitchen clatter
• Fairly easy to maintain: reapply oil (tung oil, available from DIY stores, is good) or lacquer when needed and avoid harsh abrasive cleaners. Can survive a good scrub if you feel the need.

disadvantages
• All wood will warp to some extent in a centrally heated kitchen, though hardwoods will be less affected.
• The joins of end-grain wood can start to open up if not properly sealed.
• Will stain, scratch and burn so be prepared to use chopping boards and trivets.

LI KA

...sauce

4 skinless chicken breast fillets
onion salt
1 teaspoon garlic paste
1 tablespoon tandoori masala powder
2 tablespoons lemon juice
sunflower oil for brushing

FOR THE SAUCE
4 tablespoons peanut butter
6 tablespoons pineapple juice

MURG (right)

2 tablespoons sunflower oil
1 bay leaf
4 cloves
1 teaspoon black peppercorns,
  roughly crushed
2 teaspoons ginger-garlic paste
600g (1¼lb) boneless chicken, cubed
¼ teaspoon turmeric powder
½ teaspoon chilli powder
salt
300ml (10fl oz) natural yoghurt, beaten

stone worktops

Cool, luxurious marble is a classic choice for rolling out pastry, but stone of all sorts is now making an appearance for kitchen work surfaces, breakfast bars and splashbacks. Granite – the most costly – is a favourite in both modern and traditional kitchens, but limestone and slate, too, are becoming more popular.

advantages
- Looks good in any style of interior
- Luxury appearance
- Wide range of colours
- Low maintenance: just wash with soap and water
- Hardwearing, practical and can last forever.
- Complements all natural materials.

disadvantages
- Expensive
- Needs professional installation
- Heavy, so requires a robust supporting framework
- Not sound-absorbent
- Sandstone and limestone are porous and will stain unless properly sealed with two or three coats of sealer.
- Slate scratches relatively easily
- China and glass don't bounce off it

concrete worktops

With its natural ingredients, concrete shares many of the properties of stone. Concrete is more versatile than you might think and is now used in many cutting-edge kitchens.

advantages
- Can look rough, rugged and raw or smooth and refined
- Can be coloured before being cast
- If cast on site, it has no joins so is perfect for large areas or long runs.
- Can be finished with a renewable water-repellent coating
- Easy to clean using a mild soap and water (avoid ammonia and bleach)

disadvantages
- Needs professional installation
- It is heavy, so your units – and the floor – need to be strong enough
- It is porous so needs to be treated with a sealant
- It is not sound-absorbent
- Anything dropped onto it is likely to break
- Fitting can be expensive

tiled worktops

A tiled worktop is strong, durable and low-maintenance. Water- and heat- resistant and impervious to most food spills, ceramic tiles make a functional and hardwearing kitchen surface. Available in thousands of colours, shapes, sizes and patterns, they also allow great scope for creativity. Tiling a worktop can be tackled by an amateur but make sure that the surface is level, use an appropriate grout and waterproof sealant, and reapply the sealant every six months. Remember that all unglazed tiles should also be sealed.

advantages

• Colourful tiles or mosaic make a great decorative impact in a kitchen and provide light relief from expanses of white units and stainless steel.
• Tiles are relatively cheap and easy to lay. 'Reject' tiles (seconds or ends of line) are particularly good value.
• A tiled worktop is hard-wearing.

disadvantages

• Won't be completely flat and thus won't work effectively on its own as a chopping or kneading surface.
• If the grout is not flush with the tiles, dirt will gather in the cracks. Clean regularly with a small brush (an old toothbrush is ideal) to avoid staining.
• Tiles can chip, so buy extra in case you need to replace any at a later date. (And note that a worktop needs a thicker grade of tile than a wall).
• Will need to be accurately cut and shaped to fit around pipes and sinks.

glass worktops

Though far from commonplace, glass makes a glossy, hardwearing work-surface. It is water- and heat-resistant and supremely easy to maintain, though it can get scratched. Worktop glass is generally not toughened but is still hardy enough to last for years and shouldn't crack with normal use. If the glass is not in a framework, its sharp edges must be ground smooth. Glass worktops are made bespoke by designers who usually offer a supply and fit service and who can make in virtually any shape and colour.

advantages

• A glossy glass worktop will make a huge design impact in any kitchen.
• Given a curvy edge, a glass surface offers a fluidity which brilliantly offsets the rectilinear lines of units and appliances.
• Though not a cutting surface, its cool character makes it perfect for kneading and pastry-making.
• Highly reflective, it will maximise the daylight and, if lit artificially, become a feature at night.

disadvantages

• It requires expert cutting and fitting.
• A designer item, it doesn't come cheap.
• You will need to use pot stands to prevent scratches.
• It is heavy; your units will need to be able to withstand its weight.

51
metal worktops

Shiny stainless-steel worktops have become increasingly popular over the last few years and as well as looking chic and sleek have a lot of practical benefits, too. They are strong and durable, water- and heat-resistant and – even better in the kitchen – very hygienic. Though stainless steel will show smudges and marks, a wipe-over with a lightly oiled cloth should bring up the shine. Zinc, by contrast, will stain very easily (which is all part of its appeal) but, being soft, it is easy to apply to a worktop and will give you that Parisian café look in an instant.

advantages

• Stainless steel comes in various textures and finishes, from matt brushed to polished gloss to ridged.
• Available in thin sheets, it is reasonably pliable and easy to apply, even to curved surfaces.
• If polished it makes a highly reflective surface and enhances the light.
• A stainless-steel worktop with an integral sink and draining board makes for a very streamlined kitchen and no join means no seepage into the units below.

disadvantages

• High-quality stainless steel is still quite expensive although high-street kitchen shops are starting to introduce less costly ranges.
• Essentially a cold material, it won't bring warmth to the kitchen but works well when teamed with wood or paintwork.
• Combining metal or glass kitchen utensils with a metal worktop won't make for a quiet kitchen.

52 laminate worktops

The most economical option of all, laminated worktops, such as Formica, are easy to cut, shape and apply, and they are also wipe-clean, adaptable and reasonably durable. They are available with surface designs in all kinds of colours and patterns as well as photographic and computerised images, which allow for great decorative flexibility.

advantages

- Available in hundreds of colours and designs, laminate can co-ordinate with the kitchen or stand as a designer feature in its own right.
- It is very affordable
- It is easy to look after and doesn't stain easily
- China and glass won't break on impact

disadvantages

- If it is poor quality or ill-fitted, it can look cheap
- A plastic-based material, it is not eco-friendly
- It isn't as durable as harder materials: prolonged contact with water (around the sink, for example) can make the plastic topping lift at the edges and joins.

53 composite worktops

Composites will cost you a bit but can't be beaten for durability, flexibility and indestructibility.

terrazzo

The oldest composite of all, terrazzo can be poured or made into tiles and comes in hundreds of colours and textures. Hardwearing and easy to look after, it has all the benefits of real stone but with a more uniform surface. Check that your units can bear its weight.

corian

Corian comes in countless colours and finishes and can be moulded seamlessly to any shape or thickness, making it ideal for a worktop with an integral sink and draining area. Smooth and opaque, it is non-porous and reasonably stain-proof (marks can be sanded out). It will scratch, however, so it is best to avoid any direct chopping.

caesar stone

This new composite is solid and extremely strong, chip-, scratch- and stain-resistant. It can withstand temperatures of up to 300 degrees centigrade and is available in lengths of up to 3m. It comes in a variety of colours and finishes.

combination worktops

The worktop is used for a wealth of different jobs – chopping vegetables, kneading bread, draining dishes – and finding one material that does it all can be tricky. So consider having a combination of materials: a run of steel with a wood block at the end for chopping or wood veneer with an integral marble slab for baking. As well as the practical benefits, a combination surface will add a decorative element. Don't overdo the mix or the kitchen will look fussy.

pros and cons

• Certain materials look great together: for instance, steel and wood make a good combination.
• Remember to check that your supporting units will work with each worktop material you choose (concrete is best with strong metal units beneath it, for example).
• A chopping board fixed to the worktop won't be as flexible as a separate one. Some top-of-the-range kitchens come with semi-fitted elements such as flip-up or swing boards, which can be moved from one area to another.
• A chopping board that fits over the sink gives you more worktop surface and will hide the dirty dishes.

sinks

55

Gone are the days of the simple white china sink, these days this kitchen essential is available in a vast range of materials (steel, ceramic, porcelain, plastic for example) and a variety of shapes and sizes. Off-the-shelf designs are less pricey than bespoke versions, but may not last as long nor function so well. Think carefully what you need from your sink before you buy (an integral drainer?; fitted taps?; two separate bowls?) and shop around for the best deals.

eight pointers to choosing a sink

1 • Consider how deep a bowl you need. A shallow photographer's sink might look just the part, but will it be able to cope with your giant stainless-steel pans and oversized white plates?

2 • A two-bowl sink will make washing up easier, but do you have the space for it? If not, opt for one main bowl with an extra half-bowl for draining and rinsing.

3 • Do you want a sink that is integral to your worktop? An all-in-one sink and counter-top will mean no water seepage or dirt traps but can't be done in all materials and may cost you more.

4 • For practicality, it's hard to beat a good old-fashioned porcelain-coated Belfast or Butler sink (they are heat- and stain-proof) but remember it will be heavy, so make sure the supporting unit is strong enough.

5 • Sinks made out of composites, such as Corian or resin (see 53), come in hundreds of colours and can be moulded to whatever depth or shape you require. They will be costly but are easy to clean with normal detergent or a mild abrasive cleaner and very durable.

6 • For the ultimate in hygiene, choose a sink that has anti-bacterial agent Microban built into it (available in composite and some stainless-steel sinks). Used in hospitals for over 25 years, Microban won't wash or wipe out and should last the sink's lifetime.

7 • Make a kitchen feature by investing in a designer light-up sink, now available internationally. Made of a synthetic material called Translucium, these are fitted inside a sealed unit with the lights (which are installed beneath the bowl) controlled by a touch-sensitive sensor.

8 • If your worktop is not water resistant, opt for a sink with an integral draining area.

taps and water filters

56

Plumbing is not the first thing most of us think about when we redo our kitchens, but for an efficient cooking and washing space, it is crucial to get the wet work area right.

Taps are one of the most hard-working items in the kitchen, so choose a style that you like but that will also function effectively and last well. There is a vast range, from classic Victorian to minimal modern, so it should be easy to find something to suit. A favourite in contemporary kitchens is the mono-block mixer – a central spout with a lever or integral taps to control water flow.

Swivel spouts make sense, particularly if you have two sink bowls. They also allow you to push the spout out of the way when you are washing up large items. If you choose a fixed spout, make sure it is high enough. A pull-out spray spout is a useful extra for rinsing.

Wall- or worktop-mounted three-hole kitchen mixers (the spout and taps are fitted separately) are a more classic choice and come in modern and traditional styles. Pillar taps on their own will give you the school-lab look.

If you feel like blowing the budget, invest in taps with a sensor. These flow only when there is movement beneath them (a good way to prevent water-wastage). Or you might choose a tap that filters as it flows. The best reduce the nasties, such as lead and chlorine, to an impressive extent.

four top tap tips

1 • A dripping tap generally means a worn-out washer. These can be replaced fairly easily, though a better solution is to opt for a tap with a ceramic or plastic disk, which generally function better than a washer.

2 • To reduce water consumption, choose a tap with a built-in aerator which draws air into the flow but still provides a sufficient stream.

3 • To avoid scalding water, make sure your water temperature is set at the right level or invest in an anti-scald tap.

4 • If you have a water-softening system (a good idea in a hard-water area as it helps to prevent your pipes scaling up and prolongs the life of your appliances), make sure you have a separate tap for drinking water.

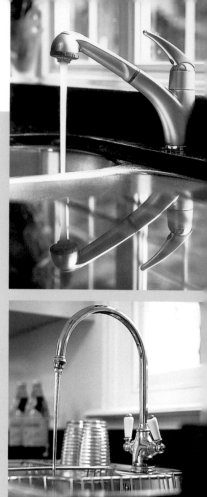

57

straight or curvy?

A kitchen with its rows of rectangular units and appliances is often fiercely rectilinear – a bonus if you are after a rigorous modern aesthetic. A long sleek plane of glass or steel on the worktop will finish it off nicely.

But if you are after something softer, think about introducing some curves. A kidney-shaped island counter-top or a worktop with an S-shaped profile will offset all those hard lines. Steel and zinc are pliable and take curves easily; glass or concrete can be cut or cast in a variety of shapes; Corian (see 53) can be moulded and stone cut. Ceramic tiles, however, would not be suitable.

A shaped worktop is likely to cost you more than a straight one whichever material you choose (cutting curves in stone, for example, means more work and more wastage). You will also need to get one-off designs made bespoke. It is worth checking the high-street stores first, however: some are now offering reasonably priced curvy-look kitchens.

all you need to know about walls and splashbacks

What with units, appliances, sinks and worktops to think about, it is easy to neglect the kitchen walls but they deserve just as much attention – if not more. They, after all, provide the backdrop to the contents of the kitchen and can help to bring all the disparate elements together. If you have large expanses of wall left exposed, think about what to do with them decoratively. Use brightly coloured paint or a smart plaster finish, or create a series of internal windows. But remember, above all, that the kitchen walls need to be practical – especially above the work surface and hob. Treating the splashback area differently from the upper wall is not only sensible, but it can also look good, adding another decorative dimension to the room.

preparation

Assess the state of your kitchen walls before you decide on a finish. Many wall-coverings need a smooth and level surface (tiles won't work on a very bumpy wall, for example) so do any repair work first. Minor irregularities can be sanded down and holes filled, but major problems may demand more serious treatment, such as replastering. If you can't afford such repairs cover up the walls with a sheet of stainless steel or even wood panelling. Tiles can camouflage a slightly pitted surface. Remember that gloss paint will highlight any irregularities, so opt for a matt finish if your walls are not super-smooth.

splashback materials

A prime target for spills and splashes, the splashback needs, above all, to be practical. Choose a strong, easy-to-clean material such as toughened glass or ceramic tiles. Above the hob, it should be heatproof, too; stainless steel is a good choice. You can make a feature of the splashback if you wish with a luxurious or unusual material: coloured or back-lit glass, or sheets of recycled plastic. Alternatively, if you want a more unified look, have a see-through splashback of Perspex or glass which will give you all the advantages of practicality while revealing the finish beneath.

leave it alone

Stripping off layers of old paint or wallpaper can be well worth the effort if you discover an interesting surface underneath. Old plaster can make for a rich and individual wall, although you will need to seal it effectively at splashback level to prevent stains. Exposed brick gives a strong rustic or industrial look (depending on the location) and doesn't need much aftercare. Sandblasting will give it a newer, cleaner look but it can blast away its character at the same time.

internal windows

These work particularly well in a gloomy, enclosed or small kitchen, letting in more light and providing a visual link with the adjacent space. Create just one window or a series (but check that the wall can take it before you start). Geometric shapes – squares or circles, for example – generally work best.

plug-ins

Map out carefully where switches and sockets will be before you decorate your walls. This is particularly important if you are using ceramic tiles or stainless steel, which will need to be cut to fit around any obstructions. Switch and socket plates now come in a wide variety of styles. See-through plastic plates are the least obtrusive.

look, no doors

In a tiny kitchen, the last thing you need is a swing door taking up valuable space. A sliding door is a good alternative and gives a neat and streamlined look to the room. Choose one in glass and you'll also make the kitchen feel more spacious. In a traditional home, a sliding door may look out of place. If so, why not do without a door altogether and choose an archway instead?

back to school

If you have an awkward section of wall left between units or behind a door, paint it with blackboard paint. This makes the perfect place to scrawl down your shopping list or telephone messages and means you can do without the clutter of notepads and pinboards. Go to the extreme, if you like, and paint a whole wall. It will become an ever-changing and very individual backdrop (and the kids will love it).

project it

Make the most of a plain expanse of wall by projecting an image onto it. Clock projectors are widely available and affordable and will give a quirky contemporary twist to any kitchen, but consider other possibilities too: an image of a seaside scene or even a recipe. Compact projectors can be bought from specialist office shops but for the ultimate in high-tech, invest in a digital projector which can be connected up to a computer or VCR so that you can show films or play video games on the kitchen wall.

the feature wall

An all-white kitchen may look clean and hygienic, but it can also be dull. Perk up a predominantly white room with one 'feature' wall. This could be painted a brilliant colour, for example, or covered with a textured wallpaper or studded with a series of mini shelves on which to display anything from ceramics to antique kitchenware. By keeping the decorative part of the kitchen contained on one wall in this way, you can put your creative stamp on the room without disrupting the 'purity' of the functional cooking area.

alternative wallpaper

If you choose to paper your kitchen, you don't have to limit yourself to a shop-bought design. There are alternatives – sheet music or maps, for example – or create your own wallpaper by photocopying and blowing-up images you like and using these to cover the wall. DIY wallpaper may work out to be pricier than the average roll, but it will give you a very personal, one-off result.

59 painted walls

Affordable and easy to apply, a coat of paint will give an instant lift to any tired kitchen. Choose a colour you like and one that will work with your units and appliances. White is perfect for a clean, modern look but can make a kitchen look clinical and stark. Dare to be adventurous and pick something stronger and brighter (see 89).

While a few years ago paint used to come in three standard finishes (matt, silk or gloss), these days there is a vast range of different finishes to choose from and it can be hard to know which to pick. It is worth remembering that the kitchen wall is bound to be affected by water and food spills (particularly at splashback level), so whichever finish you choose it needs to be fairly hardwearing.

Traditional matt paints, such as soft distemper, are not ideal for the kitchen. Though they look fantastically flat and are brilliant at covering up any bumps or rough patches in the wall surface, they mark easily and cannot be wiped down.

Modern water-based matt emulsions are more longlasting (and also good at concealing imperfections) but still won't give the durability of a paint with more sheen – a vinyl silk or an eggshell, for example. Gloss – once reserved for woodwork – is gaining popularity on kitchen walls and can make a brilliant impact in a dark room.

For a more decorative and textural result, try mixing different finishes. Alternate panels of matt and gloss paint applied either horizontally or vertically, for example, can look very effective.

five top paint tips

1 • Cover up a matt-painted splashback with a panel of glass or Perspex. This way you can use your chosen finish and still protect the wall from splashes.
2 • Remember that matt paints are best for covering up dodgy walls. Shiny reflective paints will highlight any irregularities.
3 • Glossy paints will maximise the daylight and make a room seem bigger than it really is.
4 • If you want to be eco-friendly, opt for natural paints. They may not be as durable as the rest but they won't pollute the indoor air and they are more environmentally friendly in their manufacture.
5 • Kitchen walls accumulate dirt and grease, so make sure you clean them well before applying a new coat of paint. Sugar soap, available from DIY stores, is best for this.

plaster walls

Plaster is now popular as a wall covering in its own right. Old plaster can resemble ancient fresco and new plaster is coming into its own as the ultimate warm yet neutral backdrop. Plaster is very porous though and will stain unless sealed with varnish or wax. This will deepen its colour; to counteract this, rub white pigment in before sealing. High-quality ornamental plaster finishes are also gaining in popularity. These can look like stone or marble, can be textured and coloured, and can even incorporate images or script. They must be professionally applied so are costly.

five top plaster tips

1 • Plaster can crack. Hairline fractures may add to the fresco look; larger cracks may indicate structural problems.

2 • Textured plaster has never been the stylish choice but if you are stuck with it, paint it in a cutting-edge colour or cover with a new coat of plaster – using a bonding agent first.

3 • In the splashback area cover plaster with glass or Perspex.

4 • Specialist plaster finishes have a waxed surface which is moderately water-resistant but not waterproof. Avoid using them behind the hob or in the splashback area.

5 • Use a specialist plaster finish on just one wall (preferably not the most hard-working one) to save money as well as create an appealing decorative contrast.

wallpaper

Wallpaper may not be the obvious choice for a kitchen, but if your walls are covered with bumps and imperfections, it might be just the cover-up you need. Wipe-clean vinyl wallpapers are the most practical and come in a range of colours, patterns and textures. Buy the best quality you can but don't expect it to last a lifetime.

Textured wallpapers provide contrast in a sleek and streamlined space but are not easy to keep clean. If you are sold on them, paper above the splashback only. For a retro look, hunt down old-fashioned wallpaper prints. If you can't find a pattern you like, create your own using giant photocopies.

five top paper tips

1 • If your wallpaper is very wide, paste the wall rather than the paper.

2 • An extravagant design makes an interesting contrast with pared-down modern units and appliances.

3 • Vertical stripes make a small kitchen seem smaller: opt for horizontals instead.

4 • Papering just one wall has a big visual impact and allows you to use a more durable wall-covering elsewhere.

5 • Don't use wallpaper above the cooker: it won't be able to cope with the grease or the heat.

tile and mosaic on walls

These are ideal materials for the kitchen splashback. Solid, durable and easy-to-clean, tiles and mosaic can withstand water and grease splashes and look as good as new after a quick wipe down with warm soapy water. Both are easy to apply to most existing wall finishes (paper, paint, plaster, other tiles) if the surface is flat; if it isn't, you may need to sand back small lumps and bumps or – at worst – get the wall replastered (ask a professional for advice).

Tiles are fixed to the wall individually using tile adhesive; mosaics are usually applied (and bought) in sheets that can be cut to any size. Being small-scale, mosaics will give a much smoother finish on curved or uneven walls. Both tiles and mosaics should be finished off with a suitable grout – your retailer should be able to advise you.

Today, tiles are available in all manner of shapes, sizes, colours and patterns and allow great scope for creativity. Don't feel you have to stick to a regular, geometric grid; a freer arrangement of tiles can often be far more successful: a sweep of small circular mosaics, for example, or a collection of random colours. Think about using long rectangular tiles to form an uneven pattern, perhaps staggering the tiles to produce a ragged edge. If you choose to tile right up to the ceiling, consider creating a bespoke design or, for a one-off splashback, make your own mosaic out of bits of broken china set into mortar.

five top tile and mosaic tips

1 • If you are applying tiles to a partition wall, it is best to use a flexible adhesive.
2 • For instant cutting-edge texture, hunt around for 3D tiles that stand out from the wall.
3 • Look in reject tile shops for bargains: seconds and ends-of-line can be perfect for a small tiled area.
4 • Glass mosaic will give a striking luminescent surface, particularly if it is lit from above.
5 • If you are tiling behind the hob, you will need to use a heat-proof adhesive.

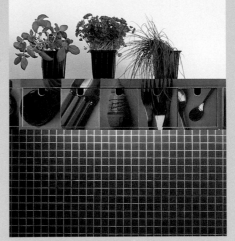

stone on walls

63

Most stone these days is available in tile form making it easy to apply to the wall with a proprietary adhesive. If you don't want the join of tiles, however, opt for a long panel of stone (though this will need steel fixings to keep it in place). Cladding an entire wall in stone will be expensive, and can make the space look too much like a bathroom. Instead, use stone just for a sleek, hardwearing splashback and choose a variety that looks good with your units and work surface. Slate works particularly well for cladding and makes a good contrast with a wooden worktop. For a sleeker, more luxurious result, opt for polished granite or attractive pale limestone. Stone splashbacks will need to be sealed to protect them from any splashes and spills.

five top stone tips

1 • A stone splashback will be heavy, so make sure that the units below can support it.
2 • Polished stone will give a brilliant reflective surface – good for making a small space seem bigger – but only the very hardest types of stone (such as granite or marble) can take the polishing process.
3 • Stone should be sealed before grouting to avoid any staining during fitting.
4 • Stone looks good in both modern and traditional spaces and works well with all other materials such as wood, glass and steel.
5 • Being a natural material, stone varies in colour and pattern. If you are buying tiles, check with the supplier that they are as evenly matched as possible.

wood on walls

64

Few modern kitchens use wood on the wall, but it can be perfect for covering up a damaged surface. It is also insulating, sound-absorbent and tactile. Traditional tongue-and-groove panelling works well in utility spaces and can either be left bare or painted to match the surrounding decor. A wood veneer is less costly than solid wood but will not have the same depth or character and will not last as long. All wood needs to sealed with lacquer, wax or oil to protect it from water and food spills.

five top wood tips

1 • For an eco-friendly option, line your walls with panels of bamboo rather than an endangered tropical hardwood.
2 • Opt for reclaimed wood where possible. It is not only eco-friendly, but will add instant patina, too (see 26 and 46).
3 • For a contemporary look, clad the wall with narrow planks rather than tongue-and-groove.
4 • There is a huge variety of woods. Browse through magazines and look at samples before making your choice.
5 • Exotic woods are costly. If you can't afford the one you like, opt for a less expensive wood and stain it. Dark-stained oak, for example, is a good substitute for wenge.

65

metal on walls

Sheet metal is the perfect material for cladding a
kitchen wall. Flexible, durable and hygienic, it can
cover up bumps and imperfections and give any
tired cooking space a shiny and professional new
look. Stainless steel, with its industrial catering
associations, is the most popular kitchen metal,
exploited by manufacturers at both ends of the
market. Available both in sheet and tile form, it
works particularly well as a splashback behind the
hob as it is heat proof and reasonably easy to
clean. Aluminium and zinc can also make good
cladding materials, although the latter does stain
rather readily.

five top metal tips

1 • Stainless steel does mark easily. Rubbing the
surface with a soft, very lightly oiled cloth will
obliterate the smears and bring up the shine.
2 • If you don't want an all-metal look, top a
stainless-steel worktop and splashback with a
brilliantly painted wall.
3 • Pliable zinc and stainless steel are perfect for
use on curved or contoured walls.
4 • For a more textured effect, use a panel of
corrugated metal for the splashback (you may need
a series of metal fixings to keep it in place,
though).
5 • As aluminium is extremely lightweight, it
makes a good cladding material for walls which
are not sturdy.

glass on walls

Ever since the modernists started using glass as a building material in the 1930s, it has been gaining popularity in the home. Solid, hardwearing, hygienic and transparent, it works on both a large and small scale, maximising natural light and the sense of space. There are increasing numbers of kitchens with glass ceilings and walls (particularly effective if the garden is adjacent – see 9 and 14); cooking and dining areas divided by glass panels; walls with internal windows (see 58) and splashbacks of glass (see 58).

Safety is an issue of course. All internal glass should be at least 1cm thick and strengthened to prevent accidents (though if used as a worktop, this is not always possible, see 50). Wired, toughened and laminated glass all add strength and sandblasting will make a panel of glass more visible so you won't walk into it. Opaque frosted glass is useful if you want kitchen mess to stay hidden when you are sitting in an adjacent dining area, for example, while glass blocks offer strength and privacy, but don't have the same feeling of lightness.

Machine-cut glass comes in any reasonable size but if you want a non-standard piece it will have to be custom-made. Remember, too, that thick glass is extremely heavy and will need a strong supporting floor.

Textured and coloured glass can bring a decorative flourish to any utility space, so choose a vivid glass splashback or seek out individual glass designers who can make you a bespoke panel. If your kitchen is tiny, mirrored glass tiles or mosaics can do much to increase the sense of space.

five top glass tips

1 • The thicker a piece of glass is, the heavier it will be: if you want a chunky glass wall, check first with a structural engineer that your floors will be able to stand the weight.

2 • Glass does smear easily. A solution of water and vinegar, rubbed off with old newspaper, however, is an effective and eco-friendly cleaning option.

3 • New technologies in glass manufacture have led to many new inventions: glass that goes from clear to opaque at the flick of a switch, for example, or glass that can conserve heat. Ask suppliers for information but remember that high-tech gadgets usually mean high prices.

4 • If you want to retain your privacy but get more light, install high windows or skylights.

5 • A completely see-through wall can be a hazard, particularly to small children. Divide up the expanse with steel-framed doors or frosted panels.

degrees of separation
walls to divide a space

The kitchen is the hub of the home and many people are now choosing to maximise its size: internal walls are being knocked down to convert individual rooms into giant cooking-cum-eating-cum-living areas. It seems anathema, then, to want to divide up the space but even in an open-plan area, it is useful to define different zones. To be able to cook and eat in the same room may sound fantastic, but who wants to look at dirty dishes while they are sitting enjoying a meal? And can you work at the kitchen table when you can see plates waiting to be put away?

In a large open kitchen, some sort of partitioning makes sense; the key is not to do too much of it. Instead of floor-to-ceiling barriers, erect half-height walls, which will hide mess and delineate space without obstructing the view or the conversation. Extend the top of an island unit to create a visual divide or, for maximum flexibility, use sliding or folding walls, which can be there when you need them and not when you don't. And think carefully about the materials you use. While a plane of frosted glass will let the light through, a solid panel of wood, stone or brick will not. Make a feature of any prominent, immutable barrier by painting it in a brilliant colour, punching it with holes (or glass bricks) or giving it a curved contour. This way you won't lose the open-plan feel of the space.

68 flooring facts

The kitchen floor takes more of a beating than any other floor in the house. Not only is it subjected to water and food spills, it is topped with heavy appliances and suffers the constant battering of shoes and feet as we spend hours of our day preparing food, cooking, washing up. What's more, the kitchen floor is also likely to be bombarded with brushes, brooms and chemical cleaners.

Most of us choose flooring on looks and cost alone, but when selecting the right surface for the kitchen, it is important to take other factors into account. Is the material hardwearing? Will it be slippery and unsafe when wet? Will it be comfortable to stand on for hours at a time? Is it easy to keep clean? While you might decide to sacrifice any one of these to have the flooring you want, it is worth keeping in mind just how many demands the kitchen floor needs to satisfy. Happily, there are so many different flooring materials to choose from today, that it should not be difficult to find a surface both that you like and that functions effectively in the kitchen.

prepare the ground

Before you lay down any new flooring, you need to make sure that the existing surface is up to it. The sub-floor – whether at ground level or suspended on an upper floor – should be flat, dry and stable. If there is any damage (a broken floorboard, for example), it needs to be sorted out before you put any new flooring on top. Poor floorboards can be topped with a layer of hardboard or plywood to give you a more stable surface; a pitted concrete floor can be evened up with levelling compound. Get advice from a professional floor fitter if you can't manage the job yourself.

keep out the damp

Most concrete sub-floors at ground level need a damp-proof membrane (DPM). In modern buildings these are generally fitted as standard, though it is worth checking if you are not sure. In old buildings, however, it is rare to find a DPM and, indeed, the traditional sub-floor may not be suitable for one (in some circumstances a DPM fitted into an old sub-floor may cause moisture to travel higher up the wall). The best thing if you live in an old house is to get advice from the experts as to how to proceed.

new on top of old

In many cases, new flooring can simply be laid on top of the old. Tiles can be laid over floorboards as long as they are stable; new vinyl can be placed over old (though if the old vinyl is heavily embossed you may need to cover it with a levelling filler – ask your supplier); a 'floating' timber floor (i.e. one that is not glued down) will work over linoleum, concrete, wood or tiles.

If the existing flooring is dry, flat, stable and clean, it can generally work as a sub-floor for whatever new surface you choose.

cable access

If you have metres of cable running underneath the floor for modern telecommunications such as the telephone, computer, and so on, make sure when you put a new flooring material on top that you will still be able to access them for maintenance. It is also worth drawing up a plan of what runs where to make any repair work that becomes necessary easier.

non-slip

Many of the best flooring materials (stone, tiles, concrete) can get slippery when they are wet, so think up ways of protecting yourself without sacrificing your chosen look. One solution is to create a non-slip runway for critical areas such as at the base of the worktop and cooking area. It needn't be dull: a length of colourful rubber matting would work well, look good and would provide an interesting textural contrast to smooth stone or neutral concrete.

consider the cost

Take into account the price of laying a floor before you decide which to buy. Wood, for example, may seem fairly inexpensive at the outset, but fitting it can be costly. Conversely, custom-patterned vinyl may seem exorbitant, but after-costs are minimal: it is straightforward to lay and easy to look after.

dare to be different

If you want to make an impact, opt for an unconventional floor. Sleek and shiny metal tiles will give you a strong industrial look (choose those with a raised pattern to avoid an overly slippery surface) and will also help to make the most of the daylight. A glass floor – best used in an upper-floor kitchen to maximise the see-through effect – will add instant drama and also let in the light, but make sure there is enough support for it.

photo-finish

Get creative underfoot. These days you can buy ingenious cork-backed vinyl tiles with photographic images on top. Off-the-shelf ranges include everything from sea pictures to grass

and roses but, given modern technology, anything is possible. Why not commission a designer to create a unique kitchen floor using photographic images of your choice?

go green with lino

Though you may not think it, linoleum – that much-berated staple of dingy hospital corridors and old school dining halls – is very eco-friendly. Invented in 1863 by Englishman Frederick Walton, it is made of harvestable materials – powdered cork and linseed oil – and, even better, it improves with age.

how far will you go?

It is best if your flooring runs right underneath your units and appliances, but if you are short of material – or cash – why not fake it? Take your flooring beyond the fronts of the cabinets and cooker so it looks continuous but stop it short of the wall. If you opt to do this, the back legs of units and appliances will need to be propped up on a spare block of wood or hardboard to make them the same height as the front legs.

10 ideas

wood floors

Bare wood floors have enjoyed increased popularity recently. Solid parquet and wide, close-laid floorboards were always intended to be bare, but now even the humble old floorboard has been liberated from its covering of linoleum and fitted carpet and is being stripped, varnished or painted.

A wood floor in a kitchen is kind to the feet and, if well finished, will be water-resistant and easy to clean. Use a just-damp mop to avoid water-staining. Gaps between old floorboards will attract kitchen dust and dirt, so fill them in with thin strips of wood (or cork if the gap is not in a noticeable place).

New wood floors can often be laid on top of an existing wood floor (see 68) but nail-down boards will need a solid subfloor. They give a uniform, clean look and – according to the wood – bring warmth and patina to an otherwise functional space. Reclaimed floorboards add instant character but can be expensive and there is no guarantee of uniformity.

Hygiene and safety are obviously essential in a kitchen, so ensure that any varnish, lacquer or paint finish is waterproof but not slippery. For a non-shiny, natural look, wood floors can be simply finished with wax or oil and resin but remember that these will need to be reapplied every couple of months. All solid wood floors are fairly expensive (but should last a lifetime). Cheaper, though less durable, options include wood-strip flooring or plywood sheets, which if varnished can make an attractive, modern floor.

• Revamp a tired wood floor with a wood stain or paint finish. They are generally easy to apply to any sanded floor and, if topped with a sealant, should last well. A covering of diluted whitewash can give a limed-oak look to darker boards.
• Solid wood floors are not recommended for use in basements because of potential moisture problems. It is better to use engineered wood flooring here (parquet or strip flooring).
• If a patch of your floor does become stained, sand it back as soon as you can and re-lacquer.

laminates and veneers

Laminated and veneered wood flooring is far less expensive than solid wood and has become very popular over the last few years. Easy to install, flexible and reasonably durable, any such manufactured floor will provide a non-slip kitchen surface which will just need a wipe over with a damp mop to keep clean. Most, however, are topped with the thinnest layer of real wood (if indeed any at all: many wood laminates are simply photographic imitations of the real thing backed with cork, composition wood or board) and thus are more comparable to vinyl than to their natural counterpart. If you do choose a laminated or veneered floor, get as tough a one as you can and make sure that it is suitable for heavy-wear areas. And watch out for water spills: damp can cause the top layer of such flooring to lift. Be aware, too, that once this type of flooring has been damaged, it is not easily repaired.

tiled floors 70

Made of fired clay, all kinds of floor tile – whether handmade terracotta, machine-made quarry or ceramic – are hardwearing, easy to clean and very versatile. They can be placed on any stable, level base and, thanks to new adhesives and grouts, are reasonably easy to lay. Make sure the grout is flush with the tile, though, or dirt will gather in the cracks. Thin tiles can be cut with a platform cutter but thicker ones need a powered wet saw and, probably, a good builder.

Modern ceramic tiles come in an enormous range of coloured glazes, patterns and shapes and are also available in different sizes and thicknesses. Think about the proportions of your kitchen and choose tiles of a suitable size: the larger the room, the larger the tiles it can take. Also, remember that floor tiles are thicker and heavier than wall tiles, so make sure that you buy the right kind.

Ceramic tiles will give a clean, streamlined finish to any kitchen and can suit a modern or traditional scheme. They are also highly practical – spills and footprints can be washed away in an instant. However, they are also cold on the feet and unforgiving – even the toughest cast-iron cookwear will smash if dropped and will no doubt crack the tiles into the bargain. They can also be slippery unless prepared with a matt or special non-slip finish.

By contrast, handmade terracotta tiles are warmer (and more expensive). Most are porous and will need sealing and maintaining but they will give character to any clean-cut kitchen.

stone floors

Beautiful, durable and timeless, stone has always been a favourite for the kitchen floor. Though cool underfoot, stone loses heat slowly, which makes it ideal with under-floor heating. And as it is a non-renewable natural resource, it isn't cheap, although prices vary: beautiful reclaimed slabs cost more than machine-cut tiles. Expert fitting for all stone floors is advised. Your floor will be noisy and heavy (check your sub-floor can support it) and can become slippery if polished. A honed finish is safer than an ultra-smooth one, but stone is extremely hardwearing and needs little after-care. Best of all though, stone will give you a unique floor that looks good in any setting, modern or traditional.

granite

Very hard and expensive, granite ranges in colour from near-black through to grey, blue and pink. It is water-resistant but can become slippery through wear. Thinner tiles cost less than flags.

limestone

Softer and less expensive than granite, the tougher varieties are best for floors, although all are porous and need to be treated to prevent staining. Prices are quite high, but limestone lasts well. The range of light colours are good for offsetting a generally dark kitchen.

sandstone

Tougher and less expensive than limestone, sandstone comes in warm shades of sand, lavender and reddish brown. It is porous and can stain easily unless sealed. Machine-cut tiles come in a range of sizes and thicknesses; alternatively, you can buy 'setts' – small, rough-textured blocks of stone.

slate

Extremely hardwearing, non-slip and generally waterproof. There is a huge range of colours and textures, from marbled orange and blue green to ochre yellow and white. It is pricey but less so than granite. Buy good-quality tiles to ensure even thickness. Some slate floors may need sealing in very wet locations.

marble

Expensive and long lasting, marble, with its wide colour range, is the ultimate glamorous extravagance.

72

concrete and composite floors

Amalgams, such as concrete and terrazzo, used to be the stuff of commercial interiors but, increasingly, we are seeing them brought into the home environment. Very hardwearing and available in a number of finishes, these once-industrial materials are perfect for the modern kitchen floor.

concrete

Concrete is the ultimate utilitarian kitchen floor. A blend of cement, aggregate and sand, it can be made in variety of textures and colours and can be polished, ground and waxed to become a beautiful smooth and glossy surface. Concrete is available in slabs or tiles but for best results, have it expertly laid in situ to give a smooth and even finish – though you will pay for the privilege. It is a very heavy material so if you want to use it on an upper floor get professional advice. Concrete will need sealing to give a hard and high-gloss finish but once that is done, you will have a floor that is sleek, durable and extremely low-maintenance. Though a staple of the contemporary and industrial loft look, a concrete floor is neutral enough to work just as well in a more traditional home and you can always stud it with a border pattern of pebbles (before it sets, of course) for a rustic Mediterranean effect.

• As you would expect, concrete is cold underfoot but works extremely well with under-floor heating.
• Concrete is very heavy, so make sure your sub-floor can stand the weight.

terrazzo

A mix of marble or granite chippings with concrete or cement, terrazzo works brilliantly on a kitchen floor. It is extremely hardwearing and generally non-slip – though avoid wax polish. It can be laid in situ like concrete (professional laying is advised) or bought in tile-form for a more decorative result. Laying different coloured tiles next to each other or in a specific pattern will avoid that uniform shop-floor look. Low-maintenance and waterproof, it is a little less expensive than stone and comes in a variety of colours and textures, depending on its make-up. Once it has been finished with a proprietary sealer, it just needs a mop with water now and then to keep it clean.

cork and rubber floors 73

Neither hard nor soft, these natural materials come into their own in the kitchen. Comfortable and warm underfoot but also highly practical, they make ideal utility surfaces.

cork

Although the butt of many a design joke, cork has everything going for it. It is eco-friendly and non-slip. It allows a floor to 'breathe' and doesn't develop mould if it gets damp. It is also a very good sound and heat insulator – something worth bearing in mind if you live in an upper-floor apartment. Most importantly, following the revival of seventies style, cork tiles are now firmly back in fashion.

Available in tile or plank form, cork is fairly straightforward to lay. It can be easily cut and glued on top of hardboard or plywood, but make sure the surface beneath is level. In its natural state, cork is not particularly hardy. Buy ready-sealed tiles or coat bare tiles with three or four coats of sealant to keep them looking their best and to give extra water-resistance. To maintain your green credentials, stick to natural sealers, though. Cork tiles come in a range of earthy tones from sand to deep brown but, if you are not into the natural look, coloured cork tiles are now also easy to find.

rubber

Rubber floors have become increasingly popular over the past few years. Synthetic rubber is available in a fantastic range of colours and textures and flexible rubber tiles are perfect for covering up ugly kitchen floors – though the floor beneath will need to be dry and flat. Once a tiled rubber floor has been finished and sealed with a top coat of matt or gloss sealer, it only needs a wipe with soapy water to keep it clean. While a matt finish looks more sophisticated and modern, bear in mind that it will show the dirt more readily. Rubber – particularly if it's a light colour – can stain. Poured rubber floors have a more durable and uniform finish but installation can be difficult and the costs are higher.

lino and vinyl floors

These two flexible flooring materials may be superficially similar but they couldn't be more different in terms of environmentally friendly credentials. Lino – or to give it its full name, linoleum – is eco-queen here, while vinyl is man-made from start to finish.

lino

Made of powdered cork and linseed oil, lino is an entirely natural product that improves with age. It is anti-static and anti-bacterial – hence its use in hospital corridors. While colours for lino used to be fairly limited, there is a wide choice today thanks to huge advances in its production. You can choose from hundreds of tones and finishes and can also find patterned lino or get a design created specially for you, though this will be expensive. Available in sheet or in tile form, lino can be laid by an amateur but you must make sure that your sub-floor is in good condition (see 68) because lino can be damaged by damp. If you have chosen a design with complex inlaid patterns, however, an expert should be called in to lay it.

vinyl

In contrast to lino, vinyl is completely synthetic but it is also highly practical, particularly in the kitchen. It is flexible, waterproof, reasonably affordable and easy to keep clean. It also comes in a host of colours and patterns. The most popular contemporary vinyls are those which mimic natural flooring materials – wood, stone and marble, for example, or even glass and steel. These can be expensive, but need no sealers and little upkeep, so after-costs are low. Vinyl does not wear particularly well, however, and can be damaged by heels or heavy items.

- Lino and vinyl can both be used with under-floor heating.
- Smooth vinyl is slippery when wet.
- Exploit the potential of vinyl by creating your own one-off design on paper or on screen. Discuss possibilities with the supplier and expect to pay for the privilege.

75 floors to make a space look bigger

The floor is usually the largest area even in a tiny kitchen and what you choose to put on it can make all the difference to the perception of space. Choose a dark, matt flooring and the room will seem small and dingy; use a light, reflective surface – glossy concrete or white-painted wood, for example – and the viewer will be tricked into thinking the room is far bigger than it really is.

Pattern, too, can have a major impact. If you crowd the floor with tiny tiles, you will draw attention to the kitchen's diminutive dimensions, but if you choose large tiles and – even better – lay them diagonally so that the eye is directed right across the room, it will feel more spacious. And any expansive design, which draws you out of the space rather than in, will do the trick better than a repetitive, itsy-bitsy pattern.

Choosing cabinets on stilts is also a good tip. This way, the flooring can be seen continuing underneath the units, suggesting space beyond, and the room will, quite simply, seem bigger (see 14). If you don't have raised units, stop your flooring just short of the cabinet edge. Letting it 'float' in this way should also help to increase the sense of space.

floors that zone 76

Given the luxury of a large, open-plan kitchen, it can be quite hard to know what to do with it. How can you create different zones – one for cooking, another for eating, for example – in one universal space? And how can you stamp a strong look on a room that is trying to fulfil two or more roles at once? Flooring can help here. By using different flooring materials in different parts of the kitchen, you can divide your space clearly and subtly without the need for walls. Lay lino or rubber in the cooking area, for example, and wood in the eating zone; use a concrete floor throughout but place a thin strip of rubber matting in front of the worktop (it's much easier on the feet) to define the most functional area.

Even more effective in a large kitchen is to raise the level of the floor in one area to isolate a particular zone. By stepping up to the dining area, say, you will feel – psychologically at least – that you have left the cooking mess behind and you will be able to enjoy the eating all the more.

make light work of lighting

Good lighting is a prerequisite for any room in which the occupants are regularly wielding sharp knives and handling pots of boiling liquids, but it isn't always given the attention it needs or deserves. When choosing from the wide range of options now available, it is important to address practical issues such as electrical circuitry and the structure of your home as well as the more aesthetic considerations. There are a number of excellent and sophisticated lighting systems on the market and some will require a professional to install them. Simpler and cheaper solutions, however, can be just as effective and are readily available in DIY and department stores. Kitchens are often the centre of family life with many different activities taking place, so opt for a lighting system that can change the mood in an instant: bright for cooking; soft for eating; focused for work at the kitchen table. A flexible approach will make it easier to adapt the room to different needs and roles.

here comes the sun

The first thing to do in a dark kitchen is maximise the natural light. If money isn't an issue, knock out the back wall and create floor-to-ceiling doors onto the garden or build a kitchen extension and top with a glass ceiling; there is no better way to bring the outdoors in. Smaller-scale changes can also make a difference: install a skylight; enlarge a window; give floors and walls a shiny surface. Daylight is the best light there is and if you make the most of it, you will only need artificial light after dark.

activity report

List all the different activities that will be taking place in your kitchen and make sure you have suitable lighting for each. Cooking requires good overall illumination but extra light is useful for food preparation and washing up. Dining needs subtle, mood lighting, but you should also make provision for other tasks which take place at the dining table: homework, hobbies or handiwork, for example. A double layer of lighting works best: one as general background light, complemented by a layer of task lighting to highlight specific areas, for instance, the worktop or the sink, whenever necessary. Set each on different circuits and install dimmers where you can for maximum flexibility.

in the spotlight

Use spotlights to show off the kitchen's good features and your favourite possessions. Track systems with several halogen spots offer plenty of opportunity to light different zones or individual items. Uplights on walls or above cupboards look sophisticated and make a room seem bigger, while simple clip-on lamps can be moved around as required. Lighting inside cupboards is useful for display and gives you a chance to show off your possessions, and you can use these display lights for subtle background lighting once the main kitchen lights have been turned off.

mood swings

The flick of a switch can make the washing up disappear and can change the atmosphere from frenetic activity to leisurely dining. It can also turn a bright, busy family room into a calm space for quieter moments. Working with plenty of bright light will make you more efficient and is better for your eyesight and health, but changing to a lower lighting level will help you switch off and relax after a hard day.

the right direction

Correct positioning of lighting is very important so think carefully, or take advice, before installation. The centre of the ceiling may seem the obvious place for a track system but it could mean you are standing between the light source and the work area, thus casting a shadow. A pair of tracks at either side of the kitchen may be better. As a rule of thumb, remember that it is best to light a particular area from the front or the side.

safe as houses

Water and electricity are a dangerous mix so take great care with kitchen switches, plugs and wiring. Do not have any switches plugs, or switch-on lamps near the sink in case you turn them on with wet hands, or above a cooker where steam and heat could cause danger. Do seek advice from an electrician on anything wired in and remember to read and follow instructions on any appliances.

circuit training

Always consult an electrician before installing a lighting system to ensure that the lighting circuit is suitable and capable of powering the number and type of lights you wish to use. Many track and downlight systems operate with low-voltage lights and require a transformer that may need a new, separate circuit. It is important not to overload these circuits.

pending

The days of a single light hanging in the middle of the room are long gone but pendant lights are useful and can look great, especially when finished with a top-of-the-range shade. Hung low over a breakfast bar or dining table, a pendant light will isolate and emphasise the area while a row above a workstation or island unit provide good light and cutting-edge credentials (particularly with glass shades). For extra versatility and a retro seventies feel, look for rise-and-fall pendants.

light fantastic

As kitchens become more versatile so does the lighting and there is no reason why you shouldn't make the most of the wonderful array of designs now available. Chandeliers, fancy wall lights, fairy lights and even a flash of coloured neon can give your kitchen extra sparkle and allow you to turn it into a more glamorous, chic or fun place to be.

plug in

If the thought of putting in new wiring seems disruptive, complicated or expensive, then there are plenty of lighting options that can simply be plugged in. Desk lamps work well on worktops: look for wall-mounted and clip-on versions, which won't take up valuable space. Table lamps provide intimacy and floor lamps and uplights can be used to define different areas. Plug-in strip lights or rows of downlights are available in kits with a transformer. They can be fixed under, on top of or inside cupboards and under shelves. Remember, though, that with any of these you'll have the flex to deal with.

78 task lighting

In a kitchen, task lighting is the most important thing to get right: you don't want to be chopping vegetables and washing dishes in semi-darkness. It is easy to assume that a single 100-watt bulb hung in the centre of the room will give you all the light you need, but unless you plan to do all your kitchen jobs right beneath it, you are bound to find yourself often working in shadow.

Worktops, cookers and sinks – the areas where you need most light – are, as a rule, at the edges of the kitchen and all need targeted lighting. Invest in a light fitting with moveable halogen spots, for example, which can be pointed in whichever direction you like, or – even better – buy a wire track which runs from one end of the ceiling to the other and allows you to place as many spots as you need wherever you need them. Don't automatically put it in the centre of the ceiling, though (see 77, The Right Direction). For more specific task lighting, think about installing spots or strips (tungsten tubes work well) under wall-mounted units. This is a good way of bringing even, glare- and shadow-free light to the worktop and will also add interest to a wall of kitchen cabinets, particularly at night.

If you are not into modern lighting systems, there are other ways of giving yourself enough light to work with. You could supplement a central chandelier with small wall lights or hang a series of pendants in a row across the ceiling. Tucking 'invisible' strip lighting underneath units is also a good way to provide essential kitchen illumination without obtrusive modern fittings.

79 lighting to eat by

Harsh overhead lighting is not what you want when you are sitting having a meal. Instead, you need soft ambient light – tungsten is best – which is easy on the eye and on the food. If the dining area is part of a working kitchen, it is especially important to light it separately, even if it is just the kitchen table. That way you will be able to set it apart from the functional cooking area at the flick of a switch (or two) when you sit down to eat.

Pendants work well over the table because they cast an an intimate circle of light, but make sure you hang them at the right level. Too high and glare can be a problem; too low and they can obstruct views and conversation. Use one pendant for a small table and a series of three or more for a long one.

Downlights on dimmer switches set into the ceiling are also effective. For an intimate dinner, of course, nothing beats candles – whether in traditional candelabra or low modern candleholders. Just make sure the napkins don't catch fire.

Finally, add any incidental lighting you wish. Place a spotlight on a favourite object or series of pictures, perhaps, or light up a gloomy corner with an interesting floor lamp (see 80).

display/feature lighting

Once the general kitchen illumination is sorted out, think about adding some decorative feature lighting to the mix. Fitting strips or spots above, below or even inside your wall units (only if they are glass-fronted, of course) can transform a bland row of identikit cupboards. All that should be on show is the glow, so make sure fittings and switches are concealed and choose low-voltage bulbs – particularly for inside units – which won't get too hot. Coloured light can work brilliantly here both in the daytime and at night, and will add a subtle decorative twist to a plain white kitchen.

For a more dramatic statement, invest in one grand piece: a sparkly chandelier, perhaps, or a sculptural floor lamp. Just because the kitchen is a utility area doesn't mean it needs to be dull.

To produce a quirky, contemporary feel, consider installing an illuminated panel on the wall, the ceiling or even the floor. You could even turn the entire splashback into a light box (see 81). Topped with tinted glass or Perspex, any back-lit panel will look just like modern art and will wash the kitchen with subtle coloured light. You will need to get any unusual lighting fixtures specially made, but this does not necessarily mean that they will be more expensive than shop-bought items. Look in design magazines for ideas and get advice from the experts.

wallwashing/illuminated splashbacks

Coloured light has become the latest interior craze and wall-washing systems the must-have accessory in top hotels and bars. Allowing you to change the colour of a wall whenever you like or even to overlap two tones, these automated lighting systems give you total flexibility and don't cost the earth. In a kitchen, an abstract decorative device like this is perfect. It is durable, cost-effective and extremely low-maintenance. For a more ad hoc approach, wrap individual bulbs in sheets of coloured acetate, changing them – manually – whenever you feel like it.

Any creative use of light – with or without the addition of colour – can transform your kitchen from a bland utility space into a room in which you enjoy spending time. A series of up- or downlights set on a wall at intervals will cast decorative overlapping arches of light; a light-box splashback will give your worktop a subtle coloured glow and make your kitchen stand out from the crowd. Experiment and play around with different ideas. The naked bulb is a thing of the past.

kitchen furniture know-how

to build in or not to build in?

Fitted furniture makes sense in a small kitchen where you don't have a great deal of floor space. A built-in banquette, for example, positioned at the base of a window or at the back of an island unit won't take up half as much room as a set of kitchen chairs. Fitted furniture can't be an after-thought, however; it will need to be included on your kitchen plans right at the start (see 15). And remember, useful as built-in furniture is, you won't be able to move it around the room when you feel like it nor take it away with you when you move house.

make it comfortable

Don't buy furniture on looks alone; try it out before you buy to make sure that it is comfortable. Dining chairs need to be at the right height for eating (you should be able to rest your elbows on the table); bar stools, ideally, need back and foot

rests. Think, too, about the materials. Curvy plastic seats may have stacks of contemporary kudos, but can your back cope with them? A long wooden bench may have room for lots of people, but will your guests want to sit and linger there after a meal?

practically perfect

Kitchen furniture comes in countless styles and materials these days – from simple wooden chairs to cutting-edge plastic and steel tables. Cost, comfort and looks will obviously be high on your agenda when choosing what to buy, but don't forget to think of the practicalities, too. Spills are unavoidable in a kitchen, so the ideal furniture should be sturdy, unfussy and easy to clean (wood, metal and plastic are all highly suitable). If you opt for any soft furnishings (the seat of a chair or the cover of a sofa), make sure the fabric is washable.

table talk

Round or square? Long or short? Choosing the right shape of kitchen table can be a dilemma. If you are after a multi-purpose table, which you can eat and work at, opt for a long, refectory-style one. These give a clean-line look to the kitchen and can accommodate many people and tasks. If, on the other hand, you simply need a place to eat and entertain, choose a round table, which is more conducive to cosy conversation. If you don't have much space, invest in an extendable table that can increase in size when necessity calls.

seats you can't see

If you are cooking and eating in the kitchen, the last thing you want is a clutter of chairs. Keep the dining area separate from the main cooking zone and think about alternative seating arrangements. Backless stools or, even better, a long low bench will give a much neater look to the room because, stored underneath the table, they will be 'invisible' at eye-level and will not overcrowd the space.

flexible furniture

The best solution in a small space is furniture that can be brought out when you need it and hidden away when you don't. Stackable and foldaway pieces will give you instant flexibility and will not take up much space. Create a flap-down bench, for example, to seat surprise guests or buy freestanding chairs that can be stacked up in a corner when not in use. There are many versatile designs on the market today, so make sure you choose something that works for you.

see through

In a small kitchen you need to maximise space, so rather than buying bulky, solid furniture, consider lighter pieces that will seem less obtrusive. Choose materials that let the light through (glass, Perspex, wire mesh) and opt for fluid shapes that won't dominate the space. Designs are many and varied from top-of-the-range classics, such as the wire Diamond chair by Harry Bertoia, to inexpensive mass-market see-through plastic tables.

make it mobile

Any kitchen can do with a few mobile elements: the vegetable rack that can be pulled wherever you need it; the bin that can be wheeled over to the worktop; the kitchen island that can be pushed out of the way when not in use. Keep a look out for off-the-peg mobile designs or add castors to your existing kitchen kit.

display furniture

Every kitchen needs a spot of display space to make it personal. Combining cupboards and open storage, a traditional Welsh dresser offers stacks of room for showing off your possessions, as does a more contemporary wall-mounted display unit. But smaller, more subtle pieces, such as a corner shelf or a tiny cubby hole in a row of units can make all the difference – even if you just use them for a bunch of flowers.

add the unexpected

Don't let your kitchen turn into a bland utility space; add a quirky piece of furniture to the mix. A French armoire can make a great, off-beat larder, for example; industrial pallets can be stacked up to create an eccentric ad hoc vegetable rack. Think laterally and give your kitchen a good dose of individuality.

83 kitchen tables

The table has always been the focus of the kitchen. Traditionally, it was the cosy family spot where we ate, chatted and relaxed after a hard day. Today, however, as the kitchen becomes more living room than cooking zone, its roles have multiplied. We may use it for working; we may entertain at it; we may want it for stylish tabletop displays. What we need these days is a multi-functional piece of furniture that can do it all. It should be practical and easy-to-clean, sturdy and stable, and big enough for your needs. Browse around the shops to see what you like and can afford; the choice is limitless.

wooden tables

Wood can be scrubbed down for an old-fashioned washed-out look, waxed for a subtle sheen (though any waxed surface will need to be reapplied every couple of months) or lacquered to give a luxurious polished surface. There are many types, from inexpensive beech veneers to solid oak and hardwoods. If you can't find what you want off-the-peg, get a table specially made. It won't necessarily cost you a fortune. A table made of reclaimed boards, for example, may be cheaper than a shop-bought one.

metal tables

Zinc makes a good tabletop but will mark easily, which is, after all, part of its charm. Stainless steel will be strong, flat and hygienic but will also show grease and may scratch, so needs to be cleaned regularly (see 51).

glass tables

Hard and slippery, a glass table won't make for a quiet kitchen but can look cutting-edge modern and is relatively easy to keep clean.

combination tables

Some of the best contemporary tables mix two different materials. An oak table with a steel inset, for example, can look chic and modern. Glass and steel are a classic combination and will give any kitchen cutting-edge kudos.

seating 84

Kitchen seating comes in a vast range of styles and materials, from high-backed wooden chairs to curvy plastic seats. Choose a look that fits in with the rest of your kitchen and opt for designs that are simple, sturdy and comfortable. Tall chairs can overcrowd a small kitchen, so if space is limited, stick to low designs or go without chairs altogether. A long low bench will give you plenty of seating without the visual clutter of chair backs and legs. Buy one off the peg or get one made to measure to match the contours and material of your table.

Stools are also an alternative (although a mass of legs can also make a room seem cluttered) but they won't give you the comfort of a conventional seat. Breakfast bars usually demand tall stools. Choose those with foot- and backrests if possible and, as always, try before you buy.

If you have chairs with fabric seats and backs, choose a design that lifts the rest of the kitchen. Opt for a brilliant colour, perhaps, or an extravagant pattern. To make life easier substitute standard material for waxed cloth or PVC, which can be wiped down. As stains and spills are inevitable in the kitchen, any kitchen seats should be practical and easy-to-clean.

space-saving furniture

In a tiny kitchen, you won't have much space for furniture, so rather than making rash purchases that you will regret later, spend a little time planning exactly what you need and how you can accommodate it. With a little lateral thinking and ingenious design, you will be able to achieve more than you think.

built-in

Built into the fabric of a room, fitted furniture is far less obtrusive than freestanding pieces and takes up less room. Existing structures, such as a windowsill or counter-top, can be subtly extended to create integral sitting or eating areas, and making these moveable (see below) will give you still more flexibility. Get an architect to draw up some designs for you (it shouldn't cost the earth) or brief a builder yourself.

flat-pack and foldaway

The worktop that swings out to form a kitchen table, the foldaway chairs, the flat-pack stool – such adaptable furniture is ideal for a tiny space. Don't forget, however, that you will need somewhere to store it when not in use.

wall-mounted

The Shakers are famous for hanging their chairs on the wall to free up floor space. Invest in a length of pegboard (available from most DIY stores) and do the same in your own kitchen.

double-up

The best furniture for a small space is that which does two jobs at once: the stool that turns into a table, the hollow chair that conceals storage space, the bench that doubles up as a shelf. Many such dual-purpose designs are available on the high street these days, so look around and see what you like.

furniture for spacious kitchens 86

Kitchens have got bigger over the past few years as homeowners have knocked down walls and opened up rooms to create one do-it-all cooking-dining-living space. Such large multi-purpose areas demand more than the usual kitchen kit. They may need a sofa and a couple of armchairs for daytime lounging, some diminutive furniture for the children, and perhaps some bookshelves in a corner for storing work.

The key to successfully furnishing a space like this is not to overfill it with mismatching bits and pieces. Though the room may have distinct and individual zones for separate functions, it is important not to split it up too categorically. It should work as one unified area – both practically and aesthetically.

Instead of buying traditional room-dependent furniture – such as the filing cabinet or the three-piece suite – choose non-specific pieces that work well anywhere and that can be used for a multitude of tasks. A simple wooden shelving system, for example, can look just as good stacked with baskets of food as with books and box files; a bean bag is great for watching television or relaxing with friends; a couple of cube-shaped stools can be pushed together to make an impromptu table. Opting for go-anywhere furniture will mean you need less of it – saving money and clutter.

87 designer tips to make your mark

Creating a functional and efficient kitchen is relatively easy these days. We have made-to-measure units; slot in worktops; a vast range of proficient appliances. Given this standard formula of components, however, it is difficult to take any kitchen beyond the average; to give it that extra wow factor that will make it stand out from the rest. Having a large budget helps, of course. It allows you to buy in those luxury materials and to have made-to-measure furniture, for example. But money isn't everything. If you approach the decoration of your room with a few good ideas and a bit of lateral thinking, you can create a space that looks a million dollars on little more than a shoestring.

unexpected objects

To turn your kitchen into an instant talking point, use it for unexpected displays: a selection of old record covers used to paper the ceiling; an arrangement of laboratory bottles on a shelf; a group of antique clocks lined up on a worktop. A collection of anything unusual will add depth and interest to an otherwise bland space. And think about displaying mundane items, too. Put on a pedestal, even a row of baked-bean tins will gain a new sculptural resonance and give your kitchen a hint of art-house charm.

batterie de cuisine

There is no better way to make your kitchen look professional than to display a vast range of utensils: whisks, spatulas, ice-cream scoops, palette knives, zesters. Hung from rails above the splashback or beside the cooker, these functional and affordable implements can become decoration in their own right. For maximum impact, stick to the same material for everything (shiny stainless steel, perhaps) and buy from the same range if you can so that the collection works well together.

go for colour

Use bold or unusual paint colours for your walls, units or even the floor and ceiling. Kitchens have traditionally been painted in light colours, such as white, pale blue or yellow, so surprise the eye by bringing in vivid pink or sugary eau-de-nil. Inspiration can come from anywhere: the deep purple of an aubergine; the green of a leaf; the brown of a paper bag. And consider creating fashionable combinations to bring your kitchen bang up to date. The best thing is, because paint is relatively affordable and easy to apply, you can always change the colours next season.

bring the outside in

A good way of making your kitchen stand out from the rest is to decorate it with materials or objects usually found outside. Cover one wall with pebbledash, perhaps, or stud the border of a newly laid concrete floor with pebbles (before it sets, of course). Make a partition out of bamboo, or even use it as a wall covering. Use solid and unfussy exterior light fittings inside. By standing convention on its head like this, you will give an edge to the room and also create a strong connection with a surrounding garden or roof terrace.

go graphic

In a predominantly plain kitchen, use one wall as a canvas for a dramatic piece of art. Buy in a painting if you can afford to, get someone to paint you a personalised mural or consider creating something yourself. If you are not a confident painter, stick to simple, geometric patterns (different-coloured spots, perhaps, as a homage to Damien Hirst) or project an image onto the wall so that you can then trace round it. DIY art is easier than you might think.

distinctive display

Think about the way you display your possessions. Remember, a graphic grouping of objects – whether it is a collection of glass vases or kitchen storage tins – will always look better than a random arrangement. Consider playing with scale (line up a row of pots or glasses in ascending order of size, for example) or create symmetrical displays to give the room balance. Stick to odd numbers of objects wherever possible to give the display a central focus.

fabulous floors

Create a bespoke floor to give your kitchen individuality: sink autumn leaves or shells into resin; use textured glass; paint your own design onto wooden floorboards. If you don't feel confident to do the job yourself, commission a designer to do it for you. The Internet is becoming an increasingly useful place to find young, exciting designers and look to museums, galleries and art or craft colleges for ideas and inspiration.

one grand piece

Invest in one great piece of furniture or one iconic object to give your kitchen that wow factor. It could be a designer armchair, perhaps, or a fantastic glass vase. The impact will be greatest, of course, in an uncluttered kitchen so try to keep the daily mess under control.

package deal

When you are shopping, keep an eye out for food that is interestingly packaged; a beautifully presented bag of pasta or ornately patterned bottle of olive oil, for example, can look great left out on show in the kitchen. Choose simple and graphic designs and bring things back from abroad. The quirkier and more original the packaging is, the better.

add an aquarium

Adding colour and fluidity to a functional and generally static space, a fish tank can be a brilliant and relaxing addition to any kitchen. A huge variety of sizes and designs are available, so choose one you like and make sure that you place it a sensible distance away from any heat sources and install it according to supplier's instructions. Add your fish and you'll have the perfect antidote to all that stressful cooking. What's more, according to feng shui aficionados, an aquarium will be very beneficial for your finances.

the power of colour

Colour has the power to change both how a room looks and how it feels, so it can transform even the dullest, drabbest kitchen. With this in mind, it is tempting to rush out and buy paint for an instant makeover, but be patient. First, take a good look at the bare bones of the room to assess just which colours will do the most for it. A small, dark room will need brightening up with light, warm tones; a cold large room can take some strong and brilliant colour. Though a monochromatic scheme will always look chic, it won't inject much personality into the place. Instead, dare to include some vivid tones. Choose colours that will work with the general kitchen decor. Orange can look great with clean and shiny stainless steel, but it can lose its acid appeal against a warm honey-coloured floor. Most important of all, pick colours that you like and can live with. The kitchen is a room most of us spend much of the time in, so the colour scheme needs to work for you. Try out various tones before you commit yourself (samples of paint, tiles and wallpaper come in handy here) and remember, that colours change with the light. Natural daylight enhances and heightens the intensity of a colour, while clever lighting can change the tone – and the mood – at the flick of a switch.

four creative colour criteria

1 • Reds, pinks, oranges and yellows will warm up a cold, stark kitchen and energise any flagging cook. Use them together for a brilliantly clashing effect or go for the subtler option by using them as panels against white.

2 • If you love blue, remember that true blues and blue-greens are cool and can look institutional. Lavenders, violets and eau-de-nil will give you more warmth.

3 • White and bright yellows are the most reflective, so will help a space look larger as well as lighter. This is useful to bear in mind if your kitchen is spatially challenged.

4 • Bright blue absorbs light so use it carefully – preferably in a kitchen that is naturally warm and regularly filled with sunlight.

bright colour

Walls, splashbacks and floors are obvious places for adding a dash of colour in a kitchen but now that every colour from crimson to electric blue is available for kitchen cupboards and even appliances, it seems a pity not to make the most of them. Bright colour can be bold, brash, dramatic and daring. It can invigorate, cheer up and refresh. Use it to draw attention to good features or away from less-than-perfect areas. Make your kitchen special with brave use of one colour – perhaps all over one wall or just on the cupboard fronts. Rich colours will get an extra boost alongside shiny stainless steel and will positively glow next to pure white.

Use bright colours as a highlight or contrast in a mainly white or neutral kitchen, or use them in 'secret' spaces, such as the inside of unit doors and drawers: the impact when they are revealed will be all the more effective. Bright colours are also perfect for enlivening tired units or old appliances that you can't afford to replace. Either paint them yourself or get them professionally spray-painted. And don't be afraid to base a scheme around one brightly coloured item, whether it is a sugar-pink fridge, a favourite picture or a collection of fifties china.

no colour

White's association with purity, cleanliness and freshness makes it ideal for those who like a clean, modern look or who have hygiene high on their agenda. It is difficult to go wrong with all white in a kitchen, but keep it uncluttered for best effect. And remember that spills and splashes will show, so be prepared for extra maintenance. White works brilliantly when paired up with the warm tones of natural materials, such as wood and stone, which temper its starkness and add patina and texture. It also works well with glass and steel, though this will give you a masculine, modernist feel. Natural materials used together – particularly wood, cork and stone – will give you a colour-free kitchen with lots of warmth. Neutral manufactured materials (Corian or stone-effect vinyl, for example) can look smart but will lack the character of the naturals. If you do go for a neutral background, don't be afraid to add a splash of colour – an orange kettle or a vivid red chair, perhaps. It will make all the difference.

91
finishes and textures

In a functional room like the kitchen it is easy to neglect the more subtle aspects of decoration that finishes and textures offer, but they can play a vital role in making the room feel right. Even if you are not aware of it, the patina of a wooden floor will add warmth and humanity to a sterile stainless-steel kitchen; the smooth feel of stone underfoot will be calming and comforting. Finishes can also have practical benefits. Any shiny surface, whether it is gloss paint or coloured glass, will be highly reflective and will help to maximise the light in a gloomy kitchen; a rough-textured floor will be non-slip.

Place different textures side by side so that they contrast against and complement each other: a wooden worktop against stainless-steel units will bring out the beauty of each; a glossy panel in a matt wall will add depth and interest. For a grand statement, use dynamic texture – but just in small doses. Cover one wall of your kitchen with pebble dash, for example, or panel it with raw-edged wood. Such bold design will give your kitchen bags of personality and place it right at the cutting edge.

three top tips for texture

1 • Use texture to define different areas of the kitchen: glossy for the cooking space, matt for the dining area, for example.

2 • Dare to use unconventional textures and finishes to make one grand statement.

3 • Mix textures to make the most of them: wood against steel; rubber against cork.

window treatments

92

Today there are countless ways to cover up your windows. Traditional and contemporary curtains and blinds are still popular, but increasing numbers of people are choosing more structural screening solutions: frosted glass or coloured panes. What is best for you largely depends on the look of your kitchen and how you use it. If it is a comfortable family space, used day and night, curtains at the window will make it feel cosy. If, on the other hand, your kitchen is a small functional room, a place where you whizz up a quick coffee and a microwave meal, you may well be happy to leave the windows completely bare.

Privacy is also a key issue here. If the room is directly overlooked by a neighbour, chances are that, however little time you spend in it, you will want to cover up your windows both during the day and at night. Try to avoid dated net curtains for daytime screening; diaphanous sheers do the job just as well and look a hundred times better. If, on the other hand, your kitchen is completely private, why bother with blinds? Unadulterated daylight and night views can be a big bonus in a gloomy kitchen.

Before you buy anything, weigh up all the options and look in interior magazines for inspiration.

curtains

93

A fluid curtain can do much to soften the hard lines of a modern kitchen and will provide the best insulation. Curtains can, however, be impractical in a kitchen, particularly if your window is directly above a hard-working area, such as the sink. Avoid fussy designs (you don't want frills and flounces in the kitchen) and stick to washable fabrics. Tracks can look odd and overcomplicated on a kitchen window; instead, use more impromptu hanging devices. Pierce the top of your fabric with eyelets and thread onto cable, for example; top your curtain with fabric tabs or mini-curtain hooks and hang from a curtain rail. Today these come in a range of materials – wood, Perspex, cast iron – so choose a look you like and one that will go with the rest of the decor. The colour, pattern and texture of your fabric is also a matter of personal choice (and budget) but remember that sheers will give you day-long privacy without blocking out the light, which is useful in a gloomy kitchen, and printed fabric can add visual interest to a plain modern space. Coloured semi-sheers will bathe your kitchen with a beautiful diffused light.

blinds 94

A favourite in contemporary kitchens, blinds will give a clean and streamlined look but won't keep out those draughts. Today there are countless designs available on the market (many by mail order) from real wood slats and Venetian blinds (both of which will cast graphic shadows on the floor) to Roman and roller fabric blinds. Most come in a range of sizes but if your window is not a standard shape, you will probably need to get a blind made to measure. For daytime privacy, invest in a blind that pulls up rather than down so that you can screen the bottom half of the window without shutting out the sky. If you opt for a fabric blind, choose a light tone for a gloomy kitchen or, even better, opt for blind with a pierced-hole design which will let in shards of sunlight. Remember that the most practical blinds for the kitchen are those with a surface that is easy to wipe down.

bare 95

Leaving windows bare is no cop-out these days; it's a conscious decision. In a minimal, modern kitchen particularly, sleek sheets of unadulterated glass can be just the finishing touch you need. For privacy, get the lower panes replaced with frosted glass or go for the less costly option and spray on frosting spray (available from most good DIY stores) yourself. However, completely frosted windows give you no outdoor views and can make a room feel claustrophobic; it is better to combine frosted glass with clear, to give you a sense of the world outside. Tinted glass, too, can help to camouflage your kitchen and will bathe the interior in coloured light. For the ultimate screening device, get your windows fitted with Privalite – a substance that allows you to change the glass from clear to opaque at the flick of a switch. Although they might be perfect for the space, bare windows can make a room feel cold (both figuratively and literally). Fit draught excluder if windows are old or damaged to keep the warm air inside.

96 accessorising and personalising

Once your kitchen refit is done and dusted, it is time to think about the finishing touches. While the latest cutting-edge equipment might look good and function brilliantly, it takes the odd individual touch to bring a kitchen to life. If you have opted for a very modern look, bring in something old to give a bit of gravitas to the room. If, on the other hand, the kitchen is heavily traditional, the odd contemporary touch – a modern vase, perhaps, or a colourful modern kettle – can do much to lighten it up. Don't fall into the trap of buying too much kitchen kit (it is easily done); a few well-chosen pieces will make the room look far more striking.

clocks

Now that most of our cookers and microwaves have built-in digital clocks, we don't really need classic old timepieces, but they can be an attractive addition to the kitchen. A giant old railway clock, for example, will bring a quirky and individual touch to an otherwise functional space, while a clock-face projected onto a blank wall will bring your kitchen bang up to date (see 58).

kettles

From classic stove-top boilers to high-tech automatic machines, all kinds of kettles are now available. The best performance comes with the most contemporary designs, of course, and if speed is your thing, buy an ultra-modern kettle that can boil water very rapidly. If good looks are what you are after, however, choose one that suits your kitchen: a shapely Victorian-style kettle or a brilliantly coloured plastic design.

bins

Every kitchen needs a bin, so make it a stylish one. If yours isn't built into your units, choose one with a streamlined shape and make sure it is big enough for your needs. You don't want to be emptying the rubbish every day after all. Flip-top, push-top or pedal bins are practical, easy to use and should keep smells at bay. A bin on wheels is also very useful, allowing you to move it to wherever it is needed.

the extras . . .

Whether you choose to bring pictures, ceramics or a display of colourful fish into your kitchen, don't overdo it. Simple and graphic arrangements of just a few carefully selected things will be far more eye-catching than a crowd of objects.

3

part three

keeping it fresh

cleaning

Compared with the kitchens of the past with their coal or wood-burning stoves, rudimentary ventilation and basic cleaning equipment, today's kitchens are easy to keep clean. Streamlined fitted units and slot-in surfaces leave little space for dirt and dust to gather, while minimal mono-block designs in theory reduce cleaning tasks to the bare minimum. But despite our wipe-down worktops, extractor fans and supply of products that 'remove all known germs', kitchens today are, paradoxically, often grubbier than those of our ancestors. Few of us have the time to scrub and polish as our forbears (or their servants) did, and even if we have help with housework, basic cleaning tasks often get neglected. Used to giving our kitchens a quick once-over with the latest disinfectant wipe or detoxing spray, we forget to clean behind the fridge or inside the drawers. Also, of course, modern cleaning solutions can be full chemicals which, though they make our surfaces look squeaky clean, can pollute both the domestic environment and the wider one (see 26).

It is worth getting back to basics and drawing up a cleaning rota. Though you won't want to include the obvious daily tasks or even the weekly chores, such as cleaning the fridge or the cooker, it can be a useful way of making sure other cleaning jobs get done in rotation (one week for the glassware, the next for the cutlery drawers). Also set aside time once every few months for a major spring clean. This is when you should clear out all the cupboards and the drawers and throw away any store-cupboard food that is out of date.

five ways to cut down on cleaning

1 • Closed cupboards rather than open shelving will give you less dust and grime to deal with.

2 • Smooth worktops are easier to clean; dirt is bound to gather in any cracks and crevices.

3 • With no joins or dirt-traps, an integral sink is a hygienic and low-maintenance option.

4 • Pull-out baskets make cleaning your cupboards far more straightforward.

5 • Cupboard doors fitted with click-on-and click-off hinges are easy to remove for cleaning.

maintenance

As well as regular cleaning, elements of your kitchen may need more specific attention to keep them working well and looking as good as new. Appliances may need to be serviced, for example, and worktops resealed. Sinks and taps may need de-scaling (particularly if you live in a hard-water area) and floors benefit from another layer of varnish. Ask suppliers for advice on upkeep and do 6-monthly or annual maintenance checks. Left untreated a minor problem will soon become a major one.

crockery

Stick to one core collection of china so that it is easy to replace items when they get broken. An all-white service, for example, looks good with everything and won't date.

worktops

The amount of maintenance needed depends on the material you have chosen. Wood will need re-oiling or lacquering fairly frequently (see 46); stone should not need resealing unless it has been badly stained or damaged (see 47); Corian should maintain its surface if it is regularly cleaned (see 53).

appliances

Most should be covered by a year's guarantee. After that, get them serviced annually; replace broken parts and check now and then that the door seals are intact.

sinks and taps

As well as daily cleaning, sinks can benefit from a once-a-week overnight soak in a very diluted solution of bleach (or equivalent). If there is a build-up of limescale around the taps and draining area, use a product specially designed for the removal of limescale, remembering to rinse very thoroughly after use.

units

Wash down the doors of your kitchen units every month or whenever necessary. If doors aren't closing properly, adjust the hinges and if they or drawer runners are broken, mend or replace.

waste disposal

Food packaging, plastic bags, old newspapers, empty bottles – today we all produce obscene amounts of rubbish and the kitchen is where we have to manage it. We can – and should – reduce this constant supply of waste for ecological reasons as well as practical ones. Avoid pre-packed food if you can and recycle as much as possible. Recycling centres are now commonplace and some councils even offer a pick-up service for glass, paper and cans.

At home, invest in a specially divided kitchen bin to help you separate your rubbish and make recycling easier. Waste-disposal units fitted to the sink will reduce the amount of rubbish that goes into the bin, but there is some debate as to whether these are eco-friendly or not. A better option is to keep a 'compost' pot for peelings, eggshells, coffee grounds and the like; this won't just lessen the load for the kitchen bin, it will help fertilise your garden or window box, too.

makeovers

If you haven't the budget for a complete kitchen refit, there are countless ways you can revamp the room without spending a fortune. First, give your kitchen a clear out; uncluttered surfaces will instantly make the space look brighter and cleaner. Next, think what you could do decoratively to make a difference: give the walls a fresh coat of paint, perhaps, or cover tired old unit doors with sheet metal or a fashionable wallpaper. Consider, too, reinventing the worktop. Conceal a dull or damaged counter-top with new tiles or laminate, for example, or – if you can stretch to it – replace the old worktop altogether. Just one chic new surface can bring the whole kitchen up to date.

six ideas for an instant makeover

1 • Remove clutter: an ordered kitchen will look bigger and better.

2 • If you do want to leave things out on show, create graphic and eye-catching displays – even with mundane items. A row of giant glass jars, perhaps containing cereal, rice or pasta, lined up on a shelf, will please the eye far more than a jumble of mismatched cartons.

3 • Repaint, revamp or replace your old unit doors. This won't cost much and will make a huge difference.

4 • Update the door fittings: modern handles will give you cutting-edge looks in an instant.

5 • Spray your appliances in a new, fashionable colour. Look for a professional paint-spray company in the Yellow Pages or try your local bodywork dealer.

6 • Cover up your old worktop or splashback with funky new tiles. Remember, though, that this might mean it is no longer flush with the top of your appliances.

101
add a bunch
of flowers. . .

index

acknowledgements

Picture credits

1 Ray Main/Mainstream/ Architect Niall Mclauglin; 7 Ray Main/Mainstream/Design Karen Howe; 8 Dornbracht: Nouvelle Cuisine Dreamscape Designed by Michael Graves; 11 Ray Main/Mainstream/ Plain+Simple; 12-13 Ray Main/Mainstream/ Patel Taylor Architects; 14 Ray Main/Mainstream 15 Ray Main/Mainstream; 16 Ray Main/Mainstream; 17 Ray Main/Mainstream/Idyom-Milan; 18 Ray Main/ Mainstream/D-Squared design; 19 Ray Main/ Mainstream; 22 Ray Main/Mainstream/Dev Martin Lee Associates; 24-25 above Darren Chung/Mainstream; 24-25 below Ray Main/ Mainstream; 25 Ray Main/ Mainstream; 26 Ray Main/ Mainstream/Architect Brian Ma Siy; 27 Ray Main/ Mainstream/www.w2products. com; 29 Ray Main/ Mainstream; 31 Ray Main/ Mainstream; 34 left Ray Main/ Mainstream; 34 right Darren Chung/Mainstream; 35 above Darren Chung /Mainstream/ Nicholas Anthony Kitchen; 35 below Ray Main/Mainstream; 36 Ray Main/Mainstream/ Plain+Simple; 37 Ray Main/ Mainstream; 39 left Ray Main/Mainstream; 39 right

Ray Main/Mainstream/Plain + Simple; 40 Ray Main/ Mainstream; 42 Ray Main/ Mainstream; 43 Darren Chung/Mainstream/Designer Terry Lowe; 44 Ray Main/ Mainstream/Developers Candy&Candy; 44-45 Ray Main/Mainstream/Architect Chris Cowper; 45 right Ray Main/Mainstream/Designer James Knapp; 46 Ray Main/ Mainstream; 47 Ray Main/ Mainstream; 49 left Ray Main/ Mainstream; 49 above right Ray Main/Mainstream; 49 below right Ray Main/ Mainstream; 50-51 Ray Main/ Mainstream; 51 above Darren Chung/Mainstream/ Avantgarde Interiors; 51 below Ray Main/Mainstream/ Designer Geoff Powell; 53 Ray Main/Mainstream; 54-55 Ray Main/Mainstream; 56 Darren Chung/Mainstream/Archi-tecture&Design&Ass; 57 Ray Main/ Mainstream; 58 Ray Main/ Mainstream; 59 Ray Main/ Mainstream; 60-61 Darren Chung/Mainstream/ Designer Terry Lowe; 61 Ray Main/ Mainstream; 63 Ray Main/ Mainstream/ Dev Martin Lee Associates; 64 above Ray Main/Mainstream; 64 below Ray Main/Mainstream; 65 Ray Main/Mainstream/ Plain&Simple Kitchens; 66 above Darren Chung/

Mainstream; 66 centre Ray Main/Mainstream/Littman Goddard Hogarth Architects; 66 below Darren Chung /Mainstream/ Nicholas Anthony Kitchen; 67 Darren Chung/Mainstream/Designer Terry Lowe; 70 Ray Main/ Mainstream; 71 Ray Main/ Mainstream; 72-73 Ray Main/ Mainstream/Designer Malin Iovino; 73 above Ray Main/ Mainstream; 73 below Ray Main/Mainstream; 74 Ray Main/Mainstream; 74-75 Darren Chung/Mainstream/ Zygo Design; 76 Ray Main/ Mainstream/Design Karen Howe; 77 Ray Main/ Mainstream; 78 Ray Main/ Mainstream; 80-81 Ray Main/ Mainstream; 81 Ray Main/ Mainstream; 82 Ray Main/ Mainstream; 83 Ray Main/ Mainstream; 85 Ray Main/ Mainstream/Designer William Yeoward; 86-87 Ray Main/ Mainstream; 88-89 Ray Main/ Mainstream/Architect Paul Forbes; 90 Ray Main/ Mainstream/Designer Paul Daly; 91 Ray Main/ Mainstream; 93 Ray Main/ Mainstream/Architect Paul Forbes; 95 Ray Main/ Mainstream; 96-97 Ray Main/Mainstream/MMR Architects; 96-97 below Darren Chung/Mainstream; 97 left Ray Main/Mainstream; 97

right Ray Main/Mainstream; 98 Ray Main/Mainstream/ Mary Thum Architects; 98-99 above Ray Main/Mainstream/ M.K Architects; 98-99 below Ray Main/Mainstream; 99 Ray Main/Mainstream/MMR Architects; 100 Darren Chung/ Mainstream; 101 Ray Main/ Mainstream; 104 Ray Main/ Mainstream; 105 above Ray Main/Mainstream/ Designer Andrew Martin; 105 below Ray Main/Mainstream/ Architect Brian Ma Siy; 106 Ray Main/ Mainstream/ Architects McDowel&Benedetti; 107 left Darren Chung/Mainstream/ C2 Design; 107 right Ray Main/ Mainstream; 108-109 Ray Main/Mainstream; 109 Ray Main/Mainstream/Plain & Simple Kitchens; 111 Ray Main/Mainstream; 113 Darren Chung/Mainstream; 114 Ray Main/Mainstream; 115 Ray Main/Mainstream/Plain + Simple; 116 Ray Main/ Mainstream; 117 Ray Main/ Mainstream.